Fifteen Ps for Every Minister

Fifteen Ps for Every Minister

Unveiling Matthew 10

EHIS AGBOGA

RESOURCE *Publications* • Eugene, Oregon

FIFTEEN Ps FOR EVERY MINISTER
Unveiling Matthew 10

Copyright © 2010 Ehis Agboga. All rights reserved. Except for brief quotations in critical publications or reviews, no part of this book may be reproduced in any manner without prior written permission from the publisher. Write: Permissions, Wipf and Stock Publishers, 199 W. 8th Ave., Suite 3, Eugene, OR 97401.

Resource Publications
An Imprint of Wipf and Stock Publishers
199 W. 8th Ave., Suite 3
Eugene, OR 97401
www.wipfandstock.com

ISBN 13: 978-1-60608-990-3

Manufactured in the U.S.A.

All scripture quotations, unless otherwise indicated, are taken from the Holy Bible, New International Version®, NIV®. Copyright ©1973, 1978, 1984 by Biblica, Inc.™ Used by permission of Zondervan. All rights reserved worldwide.

In loving memory of my father, Stephen Ehibhanre Agboga, who first taught me the scriptures. Dad, you remain the best.

*For Christian Leaders, Workers, and All Who Want
to Be Mightily Used by God*

Contents

Foreword ix
Preface xi
List of Abbreviations xiii
Introduction xv

1. The Foundational Ps 1
2. The Operational Ps 14
3. The Storm-Oriented Ps 78
4. The Reward-Linked Ps 91

Conclusion 105
Suggested Reading 107
About the Author 108

Foreword

ALTHOUGH MATERIALS on issues concerning the ministry abound everywhere, very few come with clarity and an original message. *Fifteen Ps for Every Minister* offers the reader not only an original message but also one set out in simplicity.

In this book, the author, under the tutelage of the Holy Spirit, unveils with great boldness, deft, and skill, matters that center on core-ministry questions. Ehis Agboga unravels with divine insight the knotty issues that have scared ministry students, confused Christian workers, and made many a minister shudder in apprehension. He examines and lays bare the principles and practices that the twenty-first-century church not only accepts but also applauds.

This book may very well become a mandatory handbook for all Christians, not just ministers and workers. It is, therefore, recommended to all who want to count for God in this millennium.

Dr. Bawo James
Benin City, Nigeria

Preface

THE WAR of the end-time has claimed as casualties so many soldiers of the cross. Some have been prematurely withdrawn from the battlefield because of severe injuries sustained in battle. Others have fled the battlefield as the fierceness of the battle intensified. Only a mere trickle seems to be returning home to our Lord with a shout of victory. The reason for these casualties is that so many soldiers of the cross never truly understood the nature of the commission they received upon their conscription into God's army.

What you are holding in your hands is a compendium of what the commission entails as drawn from Matthew 10, where Jesus, our commander-in-chief, commissioned the first soldiers (the Twelve) of the end-time army. That model commission in Matthew 10 is still relevant today, particularly for us present-day soldiers of the cross—the message has not changed, and the war has not ended.

This book examines the model commission in Matthew 10 in great detail. The commission contains fifteen key points all beginning with the letter P. Hence, this book has been titled *Fifteen Ps for Every Minister*. Ministers, church leaders and, indeed, all strata of Christian workers will find it a valuable asset.

Ehis Agboga
Lagos, Nigeria

List of Abbreviations

AMP	Amplified Version
KJV	King James Version
NIV	New International Version

Introduction

THAT EVERY believer is a minister is clear from the Scriptures:

All this is from God, who reconciled us to himself through Christ and gave us the ministry of reconciliation.

(2 COR 5:18)[1]

He has made us competent as ministers of a new covenant—not of the letter but of the Spirit; for the letter kills, but the Spirit gives life.

(2 COR 3:6)

And hath made us kings and priests unto God and his Father.

(REV 1:6 KJV)

ALTHOUGH IT is God's divine intent for all believers to be ministers, not all Christians minister or will minister in the same cadre. The Old Testament, which is a shadow of the New, gives us a picture of this assertion. Scriptures in the Old Testament books of Leviticus and Numbers show three classes of ministers: the priests, the Levites, and the Nazarites.

1. Unless otherwise indicated, all Scriptures quoted are from the New International Version (NIV) of the Holy Bible.

In Numbers 18 and Leviticus 8, 9, and 21, we see the first class of ministers under the old order. The priesthood, which was divinely given to the family of Aaron, was designed by God to lead the ministry in the tabernacle. The priests were to offer sacrifices of different shades. No other Israelite could offer sacrifices in the tabernacle. It was the exclusive preserve of the priests. Not even Aaron's extended family was allowed.

Numbers 3 introduces the ministry of the Levites. The Levites served in the tabernacle, but their ministry was restricted to rendering assistance to the priests, a role strictly reserved for them. The Levites were not permitted to carry out the duties of the priests. Disobedience was met with severe punishment, even up to death. The priests refused to perform the duties of the Levites not because of pride, but they were also limited to their own strictly defined roles.

Numbers 6 introduces the Nazarite ministry. Unlike the priesthood, which was divinely given to the family of Aaron, or the ministry of assistance in the tabernacle, which was the sole responsibility of the Levite clan, the Nazarite ministry was open to all Israelites in so far as they were neither priests nor Levites. In the Scriptures, God tells Moses to "speak to the Israelites and say to them: 'If a man or woman wants to make a special vow, a vow of separation to the LORD as a Nazarite . . . ' " (Num 6:2). The Scripture reveals two things: First, any person regardless of age, sex, or tribe could become a Nazarite. Second, Nazarite-hood was a thing of choice. The provision of the Nazarite ministry shows that God, from ages past, has intended all to minister before him. His intent has never been that ministering before his most holy presence would be the exclusive preserve of a privileged few.

It is clear that God also intended that men and women should minister in different cadres, hence the provisions of the ministries of the priest, Levite, and Nazarite. This was to avoid duplication of efforts and confusion. Thus, when King Saul offered sacrifice to the Lord, it was rejected. The reason: Samuel was the priest, not Saul! The New Testament, which is the image of the shadow portrayed in the Old Testament, also supports this claim.

THE NEW TESTAMENT PICTURE

Paul, writing to the Corinthian church in the twelfth chapter of his first letter, compares the church to the physical human body, with members constituting the different body parts. He explains that just as the different parts of the human body perform different functions, so the different members of the church perform different functions.

Paul further amplifies this teaching when, in Ephesians 4, he teaches that those called into the "five-fold" or the "four-fold" ministry (whichever term suits your theology)[2] are ministers in a different category. This he did by outlining the functions or purposes that this class of ministers will perform:

> It was he who gave some to be apostles, some to be prophets, some to be evangelists, some to be pastors, and teachers, to prepare God's people for works of service, so that the body of Christ may be built up until we all reach the unity in the

---

2. The difference in terminology stems from the argument whether the ministry offices mentioned in Ephesians 4:11 are four or five. Those who argue that they are four, contend that the Greek word translated as "pastors and teachers" is actually a compound word and should actually be rendered as "pastors-teachers"

faith and in the knowledge of the Son of God and become mature, attaining to the whole measure of the fullness of Christ. (Eph 4:11–13)

It is clear that those in this class have the special responsibility of preparing God's people (the church) for works of service (i.e., one level of ministry or the other). As a result, they have the divine privilege of ministering to other members of the body of Christ, who are also ministers (2 Cor 3:6).

Paul's teaching here lends weight to the view being canvassed all along, that just as in the Old Testament, all were intended to minister, although in different cadres, in the New Testament, all are also intended to minister and in different cadres, too.

It is, however, sad to note that the concept of who a minister is, or what ministry is all about, has today been reduced to a concept that is almost (if not totally) diametrically opposed to the intent and purpose of God for his church. Many see a minister as one who has attended a seminary or a formal Bible training college and has been formally ordained. There is also the view that one cannot minister without the support of an organized institution or church denomination. There are yet others who see ministry only in the realm of ministering in word and doctrine (pulpit ministry).

The above concepts of ministry are far from the truth. The reality is that ministry is a walk with God. Hence, the location, structure, or the recipient is not the ministry. Thus, every believer (whether pastor, Sunday school teacher, usher, caregiver, or janitor) must see himself or herself as a minister and should actually strive to minister; else, we may not effectively occupy till Christ comes.

The following pages are filled with revelatory insights on the ministry, the minister, and the ministered to. Drawn from Matthew 10, I trust the Lord by the Holy Spirit to teach you through these pages what he taught me that blessed morning when he opened my eyes to these truths.

THE PRINCIPAL TEXT

He called his twelve disciples to him and gave them authority to drive out evil spirits and to heal every disease and sickness.

These are the names of the twelve apostles: first, Simon (who is called Peter) and his brother Andrew; James son of Zebedee, and his brother John; Philip and Bartholomew; Thomas and Matthew the tax collector; James son of Alphaeus, and Thaddaeus; Simon the Zealot and Judas Iscariot, who betrayed him.

These twelve Jesus sent out with the following instructions: "Do not go among the Gentiles or enter any town of the Samaritans. Go rather to the lost sheep of Israel. As you go preach this message: 'The kingdom of heaven is near.' Heal the sick, raise the dead, cleanse those who have leprosy, drive out demons. Freely you have received, freely give. Do not take along any gold or silver or copper in your belts; take no bag for the journey, or extra tunic, sandals or a staff; for the worker is worth his keep.

"Whatever town or village you enter, search for some worthy person there and stay at his house until you leave. As you enter the home, give it your greeting. If the home is deserving, let your peace rest on it; if it is not, let your peace return to you. If anyone will not welcome you or listen to your words, shake the dust off your feet when you leave that home or town. I tell you the truth; it will be more bearable for Sodom and Gomorrah on the day of judgment than for that town. I am sending you out like sheep among wolves. Therefore be as shrewd as snakes and as innocent as doves.

"Be on your guard against men; they will hand you over to the local councils and flog you in their synagogues. On my account you will be brought before governors and kings as witnesses to them and to the Gentiles. But when they arrest you, do not worry about what to say or how to say it. At that time you will be given what to say, for it will not be you speaking, but the Spirit of your Father speaking through you.

"Brother will betray brother to death, and a father his child; children will rebel against their parents and have them put to death. All men will hate you because of me, but he who stands firm to the end will be saved. When you are persecuted in one place, flee to another. I tell you the truth, you will not finish going through the cities of Israel before the Son of Man comes.

"A student is not above his teacher, nor a servant above his master. It is enough for the student to be like his teacher, and the servant like his master. If the head of the house has been called Beelzebub; how much more the members of his household!

"So do not be afraid of them. There is nothing concealed that will not be disclosed, or hidden that will not be made known. What I tell you in the dark, speak in the daylight; what is whispered in your ear, proclaim from the roofs. Do not be afraid of those who kill the body but cannot kill the soul. Rather be afraid of the One who can destroy both soul and body in hell. Are not two sparrows sold for a penny? Yet not one of them will fall to the ground apart from the will of your Father. And even the very hairs of your head are all numbered. So don't be afraid; you are worth more than many sparrows.

"Whoever acknowledges me before men, I will also acknowledge him before my Father in heaven. But whoever disowns me before men, I will disown him before my Father in heaven.

"Do not suppose that I have come to bring peace to the earth. I did not come to bring peace, but a sword. For I have come to turn

'a man against his father,

a daughter against her mother,

a daughter-in-law against her mother-in-law—

a man's enemies will be the members of his own household.'

"Anyone who loves his father or mother more than me is not worthy of me; anyone who loves his son or daughter more than me is not worthy of me; and anyone who does not take his cross and follow me is not worthy of me. Whoever finds his life will lose it, and whoever loses his life for my sake will find it.

"He who receives you receives me, and he who receives me receives the one who sent me. Anyone who receives a prophet because he is a prophet will receive a prophet's reward, and anyone who receives a righteous man because he is a righteous man will receive a righteous man's reward. And if anyone gives even a cup of cold water to one of these little ones because he is my disciple, I tell you the truth, he will certainly not lose his reward."

1

The Foundational Ps

*If the foundations be destroyed,
what can the righteous do?*

Ps 11:3 KJV

THE IMPORTANCE of foundations in buildings or other structures cannot be overemphasized. The height, size, and weight, of a building are determined by the foundation. Furthermore, a building is not completely destroyed if its foundation is intact. This is because the building can be raised again using the same foundation.

Apostle Paul underscored the importance of foundations in Christendom when he warned that Christ had laid the foundation and no man could lay any other. Therefore, we should be careful how we build on the foundation of Christ.

Ministry, like other things, requires a solid foundation. This is because ministers do not just affect the lives of people but the final destinations of their souls. What we are about to discuss here are the factors that affect the life and ministry of all ministers of God, regardless of the cadre of ministry in which they function.

Every minister who lacks a basic understanding of the foundational Ps is most likely to end up an anathema to the body of Christ. It is my prayer that, as we look at the foundational Ps, the Lord will make your understanding quick in grasping the truths discussed in this chapter.

We begin with verses 1–5 of our principal text. These verses form the basis of the foundational Ps.

> He called his twelve disciples to him and gave them authority to drive out evil spirits and to heal every disease and sickness.
>
> These are the names of the twelve apostles: first, Simon (who is called Peter) and his brother Andrew; James the son of Zebedee, and his brother John; Philip and Bartholomew; Thomas and Matthew the tax collector; James son of Alphaeus, and Thaddaeus; Simon the Zealot and Judas Iscariot, who betrayed him.
>
> These twelve Jesus sent out with the following instructions . . .

THE PULL

He called his twelve disciples to him. (Matt 10:1)

The operative word here is *called*. In all the instances where Jesus called his disciples, they immediately left everything and followed him. The experiences of Peter; James and John, sons of Zebedee; Matthew, the tax collector; and the others illustrate this point. They did not sit a while, hold consultations, or take time off to consider whether to respond to Jesus's call or not. Scriptures show that they immediately left everything and followed him. There was something more to this call; it was not a mere call—it was a *pull*.

No one enters into the Master's vineyard without being pulled into it by the Master himself. To enter into it without the divine pull is to enter into calamity. Scripture is clear: "No one takes this honor upon himself; he must be called by God, just as Aaron was" (Heb 5:4). Although it is an honor, it is not one to be grabbed. You have to be pulled into it.

Even Jesus himself was pulled into ministry. Christ did not take upon himself the glory of becoming a high priest. God said to him, "You are my Son; today I have become your Father." And he also said, "You are a priest forever, in the order of Melchizedek" (Heb 5:5–6).

No matter the area or cadre of ministry in which you function, if you were not pulled into it, you are sure to have a wonderful time of struggling. Check the Scriptures; God has always pulled people into his service. You have to be pulled.

The Nature of the Pull

Another thing we need to learn about the pull is that those pulled did not deserve it. They were not pulled because they merited it or because they possessed special skills. Whatever the standard of measurement you choose, they would fall short of the minimum requirements. The pull is therefore a privilege.

Scripture illustrates how Jesus pulled the apostles: "Jesus went up on a mountainside and called to him those he wanted, and they came to him" (Mark 3:13). There are two things we need to note in this verse. The first is that the people called were "those he wanted." There was no mention of any qualification or the fulfillment of a precedent or subsequent condition, in order to be pulled. It was purely a matter of choice, a matter of divine favor. No man deserves the pull, but God has reserved the right by his sovereign grace to call those he wants. Benson Idahosa (who now lives in heaven), archbishop and founder of the Church of God Mission International, once said that God does not call the qualified, he qualifies the called. No wonder Jesus said, "You did not choose me, but I chose you and appointed you to go and bear fruit—fruit that will last" (John 15:16). In the light of these words, it is therefore clear that there is no need to put on a super-spiritual attitude simply because the Lord by his sovereign grace pulled us into his service. Rather, we need to thank him for this rare privilege and pray for help not to disappoint.

The second thing we should take note of is that ministry operates on a different level from normal life. The pull takes you to a new level. Scripture says Jesus went up a "mountainside" and that was where those he called came to meet him. The apostles left their previous level and moved up to the mountainside (a new level) to meet Jesus. This was what Paul meant when he said, "I press toward the mark for the prize of the *high calling* of God in Christ Jesus" (Phil 3:14; emphasis added).

Ministry is a high call. It is not a thing you enter into by reason of exposure or contact with those already there. Samuel was dedicated to the Lord, lived in the temple from childhood, and was used to the modus operandi of the priestly office, yet he never ventured into it, not until God did pull him. We need to learn from this.

THE PUSH

> These twelve Jesus sent out. (Matt 10:5)

Sent is the operative word here. It symbolizes the next P—the *push*. When Jesus sent out the twelve, he pushed them into the work.

It is imperative that we say here that every minister, even though called, must wait to be pushed into the work. There must be that divine push. The time of the pull (calling) is not necessarily the time of the push (starting).

> And the LORD answered me, and said, Write the vision, and make it plain upon tables, that he may run that readeth it. For the vision is yet for an appointed time, but at the end it shall speak, and not lie: though it tarry, wait for it; because it will surely come, it will not tarry. (Hab 2:2–3 KJV)

Scripture makes it clear that every vision has an appointed time of commencement. It is at the appointed time that you get the push. The point of the receipt of the vision (the pull) is not the takeoff point (the push). Until the divine push is given, it is dangerous to begin.

The moment David was anointed king was not the moment he ascended the throne. He was pulled but not immediately pushed. Jesus came to save his people from sin but his ministry did not commence until he was thirty. And even though the Twelve were pulled by Jesus, the time of their push was contemporaneous with the coming of the Holy Spirit upon them.

Friend, God is never in a hurry. He is never too quick or too slow. The souls you are meant to reach and affect will not die before you reach them. Be patient and wait for the push. However, I must warn that this waiting should not be confused with or be seen as a justification for procrastination or reluctance to respond to the push.

When you get the divine push to go ahead, you will certainly know. You will become obsessed with the vision. The desire to do any other thing will die off. This was Jeremiah's experience: "Then I said, I will not make mention of him, nor speak any more in his name. But his word was in mine heart as a burning fire shut up in my bones, and I was weary with forbearing, and I could not stay" (Jer 20:9 KJV). Jeremiah knew it when he got the push. When yours comes, you will know. To set out before the push is to set out into crisis and mediocrity. It is important to wait for the push. This is the second P.

THE PREPARATION PROCESS: BETWEEN THE PULL AND THE PUSH

The reason why God pulls us but does not immediately push us into the field is that he intends to take us through a process of preparation. This is to prepare us for the pleasant and ugly aspects of ministry life. The process of preparation is not a step in itself, but without it, the pull and the push are incomplete. Let us briefly consider this Scripture: "

> He appointed twelve—designating them apostles—*that they might be with him* and *that he might send them out to preach*" (Mark 3:14; emphasis added).

From this Scripture, we see a two-fold reason why Jesus appointed the twelve. The first is to be with him—to stay with him—and the second is to be sent out to preach. The appointment represents the pull, while being sent out speaks of the push. Between the pull and the push, the preparation process is expressed in the phrase, "that they might be with him."

Being with Jesus was the primary reason for the appointment of the Twelve, and it should be the same for every minister in this age. Sadly, many want to first go out to preach before coming to be with Jesus. They want to organize before agonizing in the Master's presence. This is the reason why there is so much talk but no power in the body of Christ today, so much noise but no anointing.

It is for this same reason that only a handful of ministers are like Christ. The rest have either left his presence without a regular and consistent return or were never there at all, in which case, they are professional preachers. This is why many ministers (particularly pulpit ministers) are a perfect description of circus-show entertainers, specializing in the business of keeping the people happy.

But why doesn't the Lord force them to stay? You may ask. The reason is embedded in the emphasized words in the verse under consideration. (Look at it again). Take note of the word *might*.

In this verse, *might* stands to convey the message that even though appointed and designated apostles by Christ, the disciples (and by extension, ministers of today) were under no compulsion whatsoever to stay with Christ, hence the words "that they might be with him." They could just as well launch out on their own, but at their own peril.

By the same token, Jesus was under no compulsion whatsoever to send them out to preach, hence the words "that he might send them out to preach." That he appointed and designated them apostles did not automatically mean they would be sent out (and the same applies to us). The important thing: once we are called, we are to be with him, learn from him, and watch to see if he would send us out to preach. If in his wisdom, he chooses not to, we should just stay and enjoy his presence. We are safer that way.

Of the people's perception of Peter and John, it was written: "When they saw the courage of Peter and John and realized that they were unschooled, ordinary men, they were astonished and they took note that these men had been with Jesus" (Acts 4:13). Here lies the difference between the ministers of today and those of the early church. While ministry for the apostles was a relationship with Jesus, many today see it purely as a source of livelihood. Any minister who wants to shine, who wants to minister life must first be with Jesus. Shining consistently requires being with Jesus consistently. That is the way it goes.

After the pull comes the preparation process before the push. The preparation process is a time of training, molding, fine-tuning, and pruning. It is not a time to hesitate or hurry. Jesus, in calling his disciples, told them, "Come, follow me, and I will make you fishers of men" (Mark 1:17). Jesus did not say, "follow me and you will be fishers of men," nor did he say, "follow me and fish men." Rather, he said, "follow me and I will make you fishers of men." There is a *making* process. This process is the preparation process.

The timing or duration of the preparation process differs from person to person. There is no specific or general schedule as we have in an academic program or a theological school. The difference in duration from one person to the next is a function of one or a combination of these three things: (1) our individual dealings with God, (2) the rate at which we can grasp and put to use the truths the Lord wants to teach us, and (3) the size or enormity of the task ahead of us.

While there is no certainty as regards the length of the preparation process, what is certain, however, is that every minister must go through one. To refuse to do so is to court disaster. It is well to mention here that the preparation process is a continuum. In other words, every level you find yourself at as a minister actually prepares you for the next phase of your walk with God. Thus, ministry can be said to be a relay race, not a sprint.

I find it pertinent at this point to recommend Gbile Akanni's book, *What God Looks for in His Vessels*. In this treatise, Gbile Akanni deals extensively with matters bordering on the preparation process.

Importance of the Preparation Process

Every person the Lord has ever used went through the preparation process. God prepares the people he uses. The nature of the preparation is hardly formal. God orchestrates the events in the lives of his chosen vessels and uses their experiences to convey the lessons he wants them to learn. The importance of the preparation process is mirrored in the experiences of Jotham, David, Moses, Elijah, and Jesus, just to name a few.

Jotham

> So Jotham became mighty, because he prepared his ways before the LORD his God. (2 Chr 27:6 KJV)

Note that greatness did not suddenly fall on Jotham, nor was it conferred on him. The Bible says he "became mighty"; this speaks of a conscious process. It shows that it was not a one-day event. Jotham prepared his way—he took time to prepare for greatness.

Also, note that Jotham's preparation was before the Lord, not before man or self. The church today prepares for greatness but not before the Lord. Our preparation is heavily centered on the other side of ministry. We take time to package ourselves—rehearsing the techniques of delivery, bothering about the kind of clothes to wear and the perfume to use, ensuring that our steps synchronize with our words, and so on. While there may be nothing wrong with these things, they amount to nothing if we fail to prepare before the Lord.

David

> Saul replied, "You are not able to go out against this Philistine and fight him; you are only a boy, and he has been a fighting man from his youth."
>
> But David said to Saul, "Your servant has been keeping his father's sheep. When a lion or a bear came and carried off a sheep from the flock, I went after it, struck it, and rescued the sheep from its mouth. When it turned on me, I seized

it by its hair, struck it, and killed it. Your servant
killed both the lion and the bear; this uncircum-
cised Philistine will be like one of them, because
he has defied the armies of the living God. (1
Sam 17:33–36)

David would not have been allowed to fight Goliath, if he had no proof of earlier victories. The victories of David over the lion and the bear while tending the sheep gave David the needed confidence to face Goliath. If David had not tended the sheep, he would have had nothing to present as his qualifications and would have thus been disqualified from fighting Goliath.

Friend, the tending process is the preparation process. David's tending of the sheep in the forest prepared him for the contest with Goliath and for the period of his life when he had to live in caves and jungles while on the run from Saul.

Moses

Moses's preparation process lasted eighty years. This was for a time of leadership that spanned forty years. His first seven years of preparation were in his mother's house where he was taught God's holy laws, the next thirty-three years were in the palace of Egypt where he learned the wisdom of his day from the very masters of ancient civilization. The last forty years were in the leadership laboratory of God in Midian where God taught him the practical aspects of leadership with the sheep of his father-in-law as specimen.

You would better appreciate what Moses went through if you had first-hand knowledge of tending sheep. Sheep are by nature stupid and directionless; likewise, the people Moses led out of Egypt were directionless, disorganized, and stupid. They were not a nation but a multitude of people with a common ancestry. They had never seen life outside Egypt, which explains the many problems they gave Moses. He was only able to cope because he had tended sheep for forty years.

Elijah

First Kings 17:1 opens with "Now Elijah the Tishbite . . ." Before this time, there was no mention of Elijah or of the Tishbe clan or people. Elijah was virtually unknown. But this chapter says this man came to Ahab and declared that at his word before God, there would not be rain, and so it was. Again, at his word, rain returned.

But, if every minister must be prepared, that is, go through the preparation process, did Elijah not go through one? Friend, he was no exception to the rule. He went through one. James tells us in chapter 5, verses 17–18 of his epistle, "Elias was a man subject to like passions as we are, and he prayed earnestly that it might not rain: and it rained not on the earth by the space of three years and six months. And he prayed again, and the heaven gave rain, and the earth brought forth her fruit" (KJV).

Scripture says he was of like passion (like you and I), but he earnestly prayed that there should not be rain and there was none. Notice that 1 Kings did not enter the record of Elijah's preparation for his initial showdown with Ahab. It was James who told us that before that incident, Elijah had prayed (went through the preparation process). James also tells us that he prayed again for rain and there was rain (another preparation for the next phase of ministry).

Jesus

The ministry of Jesus lasted three and half years, but his preparation for the ministry was for thirty years. It was at thirty that the Spirit came during that historic baptism at the Jordan River. That his preparation process took three decades did not mean that his ministry would last a decade. It did not last even up to half a decade, yet we still see the impact today.

Friend, having seen the foundational Ps of the pull and the push, it is necessary that we allow them to be written in our hearts. The Bible expressly declares that "we ought to give the more earnest heed to the things which we have heard, lest at any time we let them slip" (Heb 2:1 KJV).

2

The Operational Ps

WE HAVE seen the foundational Ps of the pull and the push; we now move on to the next set of Ps for every minister: the operational Ps. They have been so termed because they border directly on the operations of the minister and the ministry to which God has called him or her.

To commence ministry without a functional knowledge of the operational Ps is to embark on a merry-go-round exercise. Such a ministry is made precarious because it is impossible to assess or evaluate the work of the minister in question. To put it succinctly, the question of evaluation does not even arise. This is because the activities of such ministers will not be reckoned with as they operate outside the terms of reference handed down to them.

The need for ministers to understand their roles becomes evident when Proverbs 22:29 (KJV) is closely considered:

> "Seest thou a man diligent in his business? he shall stand before kings; he shall not stand before mean men."

Note that the man who will stand before kings must have fulfilled a two-fold condition: *diligence* (being the first) and working *in his business* (being the second). In essence, that man must have been diligent but strictly engaged in his business. To be diligent in someone else's business is to be disqualified from appearing before the king. Such a man, though a hard worker, though industrious, though an achiever with mind-blowing results, is not fit to appear before the king. He can only stand before commoners. Why? His diligence was in another man's business. As far as the king is concerned, that man went on a frolic of his own. Ignorance is not an excuse here.

Suffice it to say that many ministers have labored and achieved results, yet there has not been any record of it in heaven because they functioned outside the mandate given to them. Without doubt, they saw results, they saw the hand of God move in their ministries, they had abundant confirmation that they were pulled, prepared, and pushed into the ministry by the Lord himself, yet there are no records of their work and labor of love. The Lord had to confirm his word by the signs that accompanied their ministries.

Kenneth Erwin Hagin (who on Friday, September 19, 2003, took up permanent residence in heaven), told of how he pastored a number of churches for a period of twelve years, when one day the Lord appeared to him in a vision, telling him that there was no record of his labor as he had not been called into the ministry office of pastoring.

It is my prayer that as we begin to discuss the operational Ps, the divine truths contained in it would not be hidden from your eyes, in Jesus's name. Amen. The light of God would shine on you, and every shade of darkness concerning the plan of God for your life and ministry will disappear. Amen.

Matthew 10 remains our text, as verses 5–16 come under our searchlight now.

> These twelve Jesus sent out with the following instructions: "Do not go among the Gentiles or enter any town of the Samaritans. Go rather to the lost sheep of Israel. As you go, preach this message: 'The kingdom of heaven is near.' Heal the sick, raise the dead, cleanse those who have leprosy, drive out demons. Freely you have received, freely give. Do not take any gold or silver or copper in your belts; take no bag for the journey, or extra tunic, or sandals or a staff; for the worker is worth his keep.
>
> "Whatever town or village you enter, search for some worthy person there and stay at his house until you leave. As you enter the home, give it your greeting. If the home is deserving, let your peace rest on it; if it is not, let your peace return to you. If anyone will not welcome you or listen to your words, shake the dust off your feet when you leave that home or town. I tell you the truth, it will be more bearable for Sodom and Gomorrah on the day of judgment than for that town. I am sending you out like sheep among wolves. Therefore be as shrewd as snakes and as innocent as doves."

PLACE

The first of these Ps is embedded in verses 5 and 6: "These twelve Jesus sent out with the following instructions: 'Do not go among the Gentiles or enter any town of the Samaritans. Go rather to the lost sheep of Israel.'" Jesus sent the disciples to a specific place. They were not to go to the Gentiles or to the Samaritans. They were to go to Israel—"the lost sheep of Israel." The place to which he sent them was specific and they knew it.

It must, however, be said that a place is not defined merely by the geographical location but also by the souls who reside there. God's target is not the landmass or the mineral resources but the souls within that place.

When God pulls, prepares, and pushes ministers, it is to a place. The Lord does not send ministers everywhere nor does he leave them to grope in the dark in an attempt to find their way. The Apostles Paul and Peter were sent to the Gentile and Jewish territories respectively, and they both knew it.

> As for those who seemed to be important—whatever they were makes no difference to me; God does not judge by external appearance—those men added nothing to my message. On the contrary, they saw that I had been entrusted with the task of preaching the gospel to the Gentiles, just as Peter had been to the Jews. For God, who was at work in the ministry of Peter as an apostle to the Jews, was also at work in my ministry as an apostle to the Gentiles. James, Peter and John, those reputed to be pillars, gave me and Barnabas the right hand of fellowship when they recognized the grace given to me. They agreed that we should go to the Gentiles, and they to the Jews. (Gal 2:6–9)

David Olaniyi Oyedepo, founding bishop of the Living Faith Church (also known as Winners' Chapel), has told of how when their ministry was to commence, they had publicized that Jos was the place to which God had sent them. But on the night of their commission, while praying, God instructed him to remain and begin in Ilorin. Despite the shame, he obeyed. It was from there he was led to Kaduna and, in 1989, to Lagos.

A second sense in which the P (place) under discussion here can be understood is the ministry, gift, or office to which the minister is called. A minister may be called to stand or function in the office of an apostle, or a prophet, or a pastor, and so on. Whatever the office, the minister should never attempt to function outside that office, ministry, or gift.

One of the problems the body of Christ faced in the last century and which will yet confront the body of Christ in this millennium is that of servants of God leaving their placements in the body. When ministers attempt to function or stand in offices to which they have not been called, the result is often disastrous. William Branham is a ready example that comes to mind. Branham's attempt to operate in the teaching ministry when, in fact, he had been called into the healing ministry, led him into grave errors. The effects of those errors are still with us today.

Ironically, while Branham abandoned the healing ministry in order to teach, many ministers today (in the Nigerian church) are so power crazy—wanting a physical demonstration of the power—that many have abandoned their calling as pastors and teachers. Everybody is screaming, "Holy Ghost fire," and knocking people down. I get scared because some of these ministers have no business there and some even make use of "strange fire." Many are also arranging miracles and telling sweet stories of healings that are lies.

It is also necessary to mention here that several ministries have packed up because the ministers attempted, either for personal aggrandizement, ego, or just in plain ignorance, to walk in places to which God did not send them. God will not bless what he has not commissioned.

Paul, writing to the Corinthian church asks the questions: Are all apostles? Are all prophets? Are all teachers? Do all work miracles? In his letter to Christians in Rome, he admonished them:

> We have different gifts, according to the grace given us. If a man's gift is prophesying, let him use it in proportion to his faith. If it is serving, let him serve; if it is teaching, let him teach; if it is encouraging, let him encourage; if it is contributing to the needs of others, let him give generously; if it is leadership, let him govern diligently; if it is showing mercy, let him do it cheerfully. (Rom 12:6–8)

Where has God sent you to in the body of Christ? Find the place, stay there, and you certainly will grow and expand. The problem is that many ministers want to function in other places. They want to be in cities (and indeed, many are there) when they were actually sent to villages. Many ministers are spending much money to remain on television when the Master sent them to the mission field. Their reason is simple: they want to be known, heard of, and read about. They have yet to realize that the word of God, the anointing, will yield fruit anywhere. See what Scripture says: "But the manifestation of the Spirit is given to every man to profit withal" (1 Cor 12:7).

The word of God is given for profit. The word is strong and powerful enough to yield result and produce fruit. Christ also said,

> "This is what the kingdom of God is like. A man scatters seed on the ground. Night and day, whether he sleeps or gets up, the seed sprouts and grows, though he does not know how. All by itself the soil produces grain—first the stalk, then the head, then the full kernel in the head. As soon as the grain is ripe, he puts the sickle to it, because the harvest has come." (Mark 4:26–29)

Jesus likens the kingdom to a seed planted by a man. The man is the minister. The seed, which is the word of God, must grow. Its growth is not subject to the labors of the man ("whether he sleeps or gets up"). All that is required is that he scatters the seed. Once this is done, the seed will grow.

Now, notice the stages of growth: (1) "first the stalk," (2) "then the head," (3) "then the full kernel in the head"! The growth is gradual; it follows due process. After this, the grain becomes ripe and is harvested. It is bit by bit. The fruit did not come overnight. This is what many ministers do not realize. They have yet to fully come to terms with this truth—that growth in ministry is in stages (although the duration of each stage differs from one minister to the next). It is because many want instantaneous growth that they switch places. They move from their divine placements to seemingly favorable places, with the mindset that they would get favorable results.

Wherever you are, the growth you seek will come in this order: "first the stalk, then the head, then the full kernel in the head." Friend, where the Lord has sent you is the place where he will prosper you. David Ayabina, my bosom friend and associate, puts it this way: "until you are in God's location, your occasion (for greatness, for distinction, etc.) will not come." Even if you are the custodian of your church, your occasion for greatness will meet you there. If he has not asked you to move, don't! John was in the desert, and he had a successful ministry.

PURPOSE

> "As you go, preach this message: 'The kingdom of heaven is near.' " (Matt 10:7)

This speaks of purpose. Jesus sent the disciples to a place (Israel) with a specific purpose. The purpose was clear and definite. It was not couched in esoteric language that would require special skill to understand. It was not nebulous but specific and straight to the point. Jesus did not embark on a voyage of circumlocution in stating the purpose. He just said it plainly: "As you go, preach this message: 'The kingdom of heaven is near.' " It was as simple as that. The purpose, the apostles knew, was to spread one message: "the kingdom of heaven is near." No more, no less.

When God pulls, prepares, and pushes a minister to a place, it is for a specific purpose. If there were no task at hand, he would not pull, prepare, and push you to a place. God is not interested in random activity or the unnecessary duplication of efforts.

The fulfillment of the task or purpose given you is what the Lord uses in evaluating your success or failure in the ministry he called you into. For John the Baptist, even though the people complained that he did no miracle, they were quick to acknowledge that all he said about Jesus was true (John 10:40–42) and as such, many of them believed in Jesus.

Within the framework of objectivity, John fulfilled the purpose for which he was sent—*to prepare the way ahead of Christ*. He did it successfully such that, even though he never opened a blind eye or unstopped a deaf ear, he fulfilled the divine mandate given him. Hear Jesus's testimony about him:

> After John's messengers left, Jesus began to speak to the crowd about John, "What did you go out into the desert to see? A reed swayed by the wind? If not, what did you go out to see? A man dressed in fine clothes? No, those who wear expensive clothes and indulge in luxury are in palaces. But what did you go out to see? A prophet? Yes, I tell you, and more than a prophet. This is the one about whom it is written: 'I will send my messenger ahead of you, who will prepare your way before you.' " (Luke 7:24–27)

Jesus said John was more than a prophet, but he did no miracle. Why then was he more than a prophet? He knew the purpose for which he was sent, and he fulfilled it.

Myles Munroe, founder and president of the Bahamas Faith Ministries International and motivational speaker of international repute, has said that wherever purpose is not known, abuse is inevitable. Ignorance of the divine purpose(s) of God for their lives and ministries has caused many a minister to abuse the grace and anointing of God upon their lives. Many are laboring without seeing results; they see no significant breakthrough in the ministry simply because they do not know the purpose of the call or have deviated from it. Others have been termed (or have termed themselves) failures simply because they have no large followings, have not performed any miraculous sign, have no posh cars, no swanky wardrobes, no fat bank accounts, no exquisite duplexes, and amazingly, no beautiful faces to drool over! Success in ministry is not measured by these things but by the fulfillment of the purpose for which we were pulled.

I get disgusted when we measure success in ministry in the realm of the physical. We are told: "lack of crowd is lack of compassion and anointing," such that many ministers would do anything to get the crowd even if it means employing occult and subterranean measures. God sent Ezekiel but warned that the people would not believe and accept his message (Ezek 2—3:9). Had Ezekiel lived in our day, he would have no mammoth crowd, only a handful of people would follow him. Our generation, holding rigidly to the theory of "your class determines your crowd and your crowd, your crown (reward)," would declare Ezekiel a failure. Although we would counsel "Bishop" Ezekiel to search himself for any known sin, or to battle the unseen spiritual forces against his ministry, or better still, quit ministry, God and all of heaven would declare him a worthy general, faithful in all ramifications.

Admittedly, there is nothing primarily wrong with having the crowd. Numerical increase is one of the indices of a healthy ministry. Most importantly, the crowds were a significant feature of the ministry of Jesus on earth (even a casual reading of the gospels would reveal this). But, what is both scary and appalling is the frightening dimensions to which the importance of the crowd has been elevated. Even the Lord himself did not attach the level of importance (and hype) that the twenty-first-century church has come to attach to the crowd. He was more concerned with the pursuit and fulfillment of his purpose.

All ministers, no matter the cadre of ministry, whether as pastor, teacher, usher, custodian, or caregiver, should know the purpose for which they are called and sent to a place. At least, they should be able to define the purpose in one sentence, at most two, or at the very extreme, in one paragraph. The purpose for which Jesus sent out the disciples was simple and one sentence long: "The kingdom of heaven is near." Yours shouldn't be different.

Dear minister, the pursuit of purpose is what will make you. The Scripture is clear: "Seest thou a man diligent in his business? he shall stand before kings; he shall not stand before mean men." Paul knew this, and therefore charged those under him to pursue the fulfillment of the purposes of God for their lives and ministries, writing, "Tell Archippus: 'See to it that you complete the work you have received in the Lord' " (Col 4:17). He reminded Titus: "The reason I left you in Crete was that you might straighten what was left unfinished and appoint elders in every town, as I directed you" (Titus 1:5). And for Timothy: "As I urged you when I went into Macedonia, stay there in Ephesus so that you may command certain men not to teach false doctrines any longer, not to devote themselves to myths and endless genealogies" (1 Tim 1:3–4).

Sadly, the body of Christ is filled with a large number of men who have abandoned the purpose for which God pulled, prepared, and pushed them into his service. Paul's primary purpose was to reach the Gentiles. If Paul had contacted the Jews in the course of ministering to the Gentiles, he would have shared the gospel with them, but Paul would not abandon the primary assignment of reaching the Gentiles to pursue the Jews. If he had done that, the Jews no doubt would be saved, but as far as heaven is concerned, he would be a failure because he labored in someone else's vineyard.

The Pursuit of Purpose: The Goals Connection

The pursuit of purpose will necessitate the setting of goals to ensure its fulfillment. Goals are designed and set in line with purposes, that is, towards the fulfillment of the overall purpose to be achieved.

At a Student Christian Movement Leaders Seminar I attended years ago, I learned that there are three basic types of goals: high-priority goals, maintenance-status goals, and deferred goals.

High Priority Goals

High-priority goals are designed and set in line with the purpose for which the organization was set up. The leader sets the high-priority goals and strives to accomplish them. Attaining these goals automatically means attaining the purpose for which the organization was set up. High-priority goals are often seen or expressed in the pet projects and innovations of leaders. Hence, they are pursued diligently, unless the leader does not intend to carve a niche for himself.

Maintenance-Status Goals

Maintenance-status goals are set to maintain the structure and machinery of the organization already in place. They will not only ensure the organization's continued relevance and usefulness but also guarantee a smooth running of the organization. The programs and projects under maintenance-status goals first begin as high-priority goals. They are transferred into the maintenance-status category upon their attainment and complete integration into the activities of the organization. At this point, the organization is set to begin breaking new grounds (pursuing new high-priority goals). As such, maintenance-status goals are necessarily incidental to the effective pursuit and attainment of high priority goals. They are pursued and funded as recurrent expenditures.

The difference between high-priority goals and maintenance-status goals is that, while projects under the former are in most cases novel and are funded by capital expenditure, the latter is not. However, the latter is pursued in order to prevent a breakdown of existing infrastructure and machinery, so as not to cripple the pursuit of the high-priority goals.

Deferred Goals

Deferred goals are those goals, which, though in line with the overall purpose or the mission statement of the organization, are not feasible in the present. That is, the prevailing situation and circumstances do not favor their pursuit. The programs and projects under this goal should be drawn into proposals and stored in files tagged "Keep In View" (KIV). This is to ensure that when such projects become feasible, the proposals can be reached with ease and pursued. Every sensible leader would pursue the attainment of high-priority goals; only foolish leaders would concentrate on the pursuit of deferred goals when the situation does not permit.

These goal-types are necessary in the pursuit of the purpose for which every minister has been called. High-priority goals are the primary assignments the minister must pursue in order to fulfill his calling. Maintenance-status goals are those goals the minister must strive to keep in place, if he is to pursue the high-priority goals without (or with minimum) distraction. Deferred goals are those goals that are beneficial or necessary for the ministry, but the minister has not been called to do them or has no direct leading to pursue them now. There is no such thing as, "we can do it now by faith" in this regard. God is a God of process; he is not a God of confusion.

David Oyedepo has told of how he knew in the 1980s when his ministry was starting off that they would own a jet and build the record-setting fifty-thousand-seat auditorium. But they did nothing about it then, because the situation on the ground did not permit it. Back then, these projects were deferred goals. Later, during their pursuit, they became high-priority goals. Today, having been completed, they now belong to the maintenance-status category.

General and Specific Purpose

Finally, the purpose of ministry can be split into two broad categories: *general purpose* and *specific purpose*.

GENERAL PURPOSE

The scriptural basis for general purpose is found in these Scriptures:

> Therefore go and make disciples of all nations, baptizing them in the name of the Father and of the Son and of the Holy Spirit and teaching them to obey everything I have commanded you. And surely I am with you always, to the very end of the age. (Matt 28:19–20)

> All this is from God, who reconciled us to himself through Christ and gave us the ministry of reconciliation: that God was reconciling the world to himself in Christ, not counting men's sins against them. And he has committed to us the message of reconciliation. (2 Cor 5:18–19)

In these two Scriptures is set the general purpose of God for pulling men into ministry. That purpose is to save and disciple the sinner, so that he or she, in turn, can save and disciple others. Whatever a minister may preach and teach, whatever structure a minister may put in place, if it will not lead to the salvation of others and their being discipled to become instruments in the hands of God to save others, then, sad to say, that minister (no matter the size of the crowd gathered, no matter the physical success) has missed the mark—that minister has missed the overall purpose of his or her calling for ministry.

Jesus knew the overall purpose of his calling, such that when he was accused, he replied, "I am not come to call the righteous, but sinners to repentance" (Luke 5:32). Jesus did so many things on earth. He taught prosperity principles, taught on marriage, on good neighborliness, deliverance, and civil obedience. But it was all geared at one thing: to call the sinner to repentance.

I've heard preachers say, "I have been called to teach prosperity and no more." So they refuse to teach their flock other scriptural truths and end up raising wealthy men who may burn in hell. This is the reason why we have so many malnourished Christians. That's why there are many "Christians" without a personal knowledge of Jesus.

Whatever you have been called to preach or teach to the body of Christ, whatever your vision, or mission, if it will not lead the sinner to the cross in repentance, if it will not restore the backslider and edify the believer, something is *wrong* with your message, your calling. Check whether you are not preaching another gospel.

Specific Purpose

The specific purpose is the second category into which the purpose for ministry can be divided.

> The reason I left you in Crete was that you might straighten out what was left unfinished and appoint elders in every town, as I directed you. (Titus 1:5)

> As I urged you when I went into Macedonia, stay there in Ephesus so that you may command certain men not to teach false doctrine any longer nor to devote themselves to myths and endless genealogies. (1 Tim 1:3–4)

In these passages of Scripture, we see the specific reasons why Titus and Timothy were left in Crete and Ephesus respectively. They were given specific assignments to accomplish. Titus was to straighten out unfinished business and appoint elders, and Timothy was to ensure that certain men ceased from promoting false doctrines. But apart from these assignments, they were also required to do other things necessary for the spiritual well-being of the churches in their care.

The situation is not different today. God still calls people to carry out specific assignments. If they fail in it, they fail in their primary assignment. When you hear people talk of their commission or the mandate they received from the Lord, they are talking about the specific purpose for which they were pulled. But then, the execution of this specific purpose must be in line with the attainment of the general purpose; the relationship between both general and specific purpose must be pari passu.

As we close this discourse on purpose in the life and ministry of every minister, it is pertinent, at this stage, that you identify in clear terms God's purpose for pulling and pushing you into ministry and determine the extent to which you have pursued and are willing to pursue it.

POWER

> Heal the sick, raise the dead, cleanse those who have leprosy, drive out demons. Freely you have received, freely give. (Matt 10:8)

Matthew 10:8 speaks of power. It talks of the different ways in which the power of God is manifested. For every minister that God has pulled, prepared, pushed, and placed in a location to fulfill a divine purpose, there is divine power available. This power is made available to ensure and guarantee the success of the person sent. However, many ministers do not know the power made available to them. Hence, many are trying to make a success of ministry by their own strength. But Scripture is clear: "For by strength shall no man prevail" (1 Sam 2:9). Others know the power available, but they are in the wrong place, so nothing happens. Some, who know the power and are in the right place, are ignorant of the purpose of their call. Those who possess the knowledge lack the prerequisite keys of holiness and faith.

Friend, God does not pull us into his service to disgrace us. When God pulls us, he backs us up. He gives us the divine enablement to succeed. Jesus told his disciples:

> I have given you authority to trample on snakes and scorpions and to overcome all the power of the enemy; nothing will harm you. (Luke 10:19)

> And these signs will accompany those who believe: In my name, they will drive out demons; they will speak in new tongues; they will pick up serpents with their hands; and when they drink deadly poison, it will not hurt them at all; they will place their hands on sick people and they will get well. (Mark 16:17–19)

This is *power*! This same power is still available for all, for all who have been called, for all who believe! Scripture teaches clearly that this power has not only been given to us but is in us (the church).

> Now to him who is able to do immeasurably more than all we ask or imagine, according to his power that is at work *within* us. (Eph 3:20; emphasis added)

Why is this power given? For what purpose? The word of God is clear.

> His intent was that now through the church, the manifold wisdom of God should be made known to the rulers and authorities in the heavenly realms, according to his eternal purpose which he accomplished in Christ Jesus our Lord. (Eph 3:10–11)

This power is given that we may display the wisdom of God, which Scripture says, is manifold, to the rulers and authorities in the heavenly realms. This power is not to destroy people; God wants their souls saved. It is not for personal aggrandizement; thus, Scripture says: "Freely you have received, freely give."

Some have argued that this power is not extant in this dispensation. Scripture, however, is clear on this: "And these signs will accompany those who believe." Anyone who believes will see signs. This promise was not restricted. Peter confirms it in Acts 2:39: "This promise is for you and your children and for all who are far off—for all whom the Lord our God will call." If we are not in the class of "you," or in the class of "your children," we should be in the class of "all who are far off," and if we are too far off to be included there, we most certainly belong to the class of "all whom the Lord our God will call"—because He has called us (1 Pet 2:9).

Furthermore, in John 14:12–14 Jesus himself declared:

> I tell you the truth, anyone who has faith in me will do what I have been doing. He will do even greater things than these, because I am going to the Father. And I will do whatever you ask in my name, so that the Son may bring glory to the Father. You may ask me for anything in my name, and I will do it.

According to our Lord, we will not only do what he did; we will do greater things. Please notice that we only require faith to do the things he did, but we do not require faith to do greater things. Greater things will be done, not by faith, but because he has gone to be with the Father—and he is with him now!

Jesus in this same passage gives us the key to achievement—his name. Anything we ask in his name will be done. "You may ask me for *anything* in my name, and I will do it." Anything means anything; it includes everything without exception. This is power! It means we will open blind eyes, unstop deaf ears, unlock dumb tongues, heal lame and crippled legs, raise the dead, heal AIDS and other sicknesses and diseases, deliver men from insanity and drug addiction, decree things and they will come to pass. Anything, Jesus said, if only we ask in his name.

But why his name? The Bible teaches that God has highly exalted Jesus and given him a name above every other name, that "at the name of Jesus, every knee must bow; in heaven and on earth and under the earth" (Phil 2:9-11).

So friend, you can do it! This promise was not made only to pastors, evangelists, and apostles. It was not made only to white preachers. As you can see from the Scriptures, there was no class restriction. The next time a sick or diseased person is brought to you, pray in the name of Jesus and you will see the person healed! When people with problems come to you, in two or three sentences, proclaim the problem solved in the name of Jesus, and it will be done. The name of Jesus is credit—worthy, any time, any day, anywhere! God can pay his bills!

I was getting ready to go out when Frank T. came to see me on October 19, 2000, in my residence off campus. His course adviser had told him that he owed the department some courses. When given the list of courses, he discovered that he had passed some of them, but the results were not entered into his file. He started the process of amending the records but the head of the department refused to enter the grades. The matter kept dragging on. Frank became so disillusioned because of the possibility of having to enroll in another session. After narrating his ordeal, I prayed with him for about three minutes and declared the problem solved.

You won't believe it, but that same day, Frank went back there, and in the midst of the large number of students with similar problems, the head of the department stood up, beckoned to Frank to come over, and asked what the problem was. When Frank told him, he went over to the outer office, picked up Frank's file, entered the grades as Frank mentioned them (without checking them out), and signed against them, much against the regulations. Then, he turned to the rest of the students and addressed them, "Let none of you accuse me of not wanting you to graduate. As you can see, I have just helped one of you. Now everyone should leave my office; I have work to do." Frank couldn't believe it! He was all joy when he narrated this event to me the following night, and we blessed the Lord.

One night early in July 2000, I had a dream. In that dream, I was at the funeral ceremony of a classmate who died and was buried in the month of June. But in this dream, as the corpse was being interred, I discovered that rather than this late classmate, I saw Amos, a member of our fellowship who was then on internship for fourth-year students in the

Faculty of Agriculture. I woke up. Though I prayed immediately, I had heaviness within me and so that afternoon, I called three other leaders and we prayed that night. We cancelled every spirit of death around Amos. We took authority and declared that Amos shall not, will not, and must not die. At the time of praying, not one of us knew where Amos was. All we knew was that like every other fourth-year agriculture student, he had gone for field posting.

After his return, none of us asked him. In fact, I had forgotten that we even prayed for him. But on October 28, during the birthday celebration of one of our sisters, Amos decided to share a testimony. Hear him:

> I went for my field practical training at Idomor fish farm, Olomoro, Delta state. We were about eleven boys in a room and parlor. It happened that at the time of our visit, there was no light in the village, hence we were given a power plant that would work for some hours before being put off. I needed to read at night, so I bought candles. A certain night, I lit one, kept it on a plastic container near my head, and started reading. However, I slept off, and behold the candle melted and ignited the plastic container. Everything around me got burnt including part of my pillow. The lives of eleven powerfully built boys were in danger. But God in his infinite mercy delivered all of us . . . though things were destroyed, no life was hurt.

After the testimony, I told him to get ready to share this same testimony the following day (Sunday, October 29) in fellowship. He did, and I narrated how the Lord had revealed what was to happen and how four of us had prayed. Friend, the power of God is great, and time and space do not limit it.

Let me share with you another of the amazing testimonies of the working of God's power I have seen in my little walk and work with God. On September 15, 1999, I was preaching at the University of Benin, Ugbowo campus on the topic of convincing proofs from Acts 1:3. At the close of the message, I called for all those with problems that had defied all solutions. I began to pray with each person that had come forward. There was this particular lady, a final-year law student, who had had blisters on her palms since she was four. She had been prayed for in other places. I just prayed with her in faith. Then on December 12, 1999, she gave her testimony, that after the meeting of September 15, the Lord miraculously healed her. It was during the testimony she described the pain and problems those blisters had given her. She then raised her hand for all to see that those blisters were no longer there. They were gone. Gone forever, never to return again.

The Receipt of Power

The most frequently asked question is, "How do I receive and keep this power?" So much material on this abounds everywhere, particularly those by the ministry greats. However, we shall quickly look at a few things. Jesus told us: "But you will receive power when the Holy Spirit comes on you; and you will be my witnesses in Jerusalem, and in all Judea and Samaria, and to the ends of the earth" (Acts 1:8). It is clear that power is received when the Holy Spirit comes.

It is also clear from this Scripture that the Holy Spirit is not the power. But power is given by virtue of the Holy Spirit's coming upon the believer. Those who teach that the Holy Spirit is the power unwittingly deny the personality of the Holy Spirit, thereby reducing him to a force or a concept. He is a person, the third in the Godhead. John 16 is a clear example of a Scripture that teaches strongly the personality (or personhood) of the Holy Spirit.

Let's look at Scriptures to prove that the Holy Spirit is separate from the power.

"Jesus, *full* of the Holy Spirit, returned from the Jordan and was led by the Spirit in the desert" (Luke 4:1; emphasis added). Note that Jesus was *full* of the Holy Spirit, not with power. Remember, Jesus taught the apostles that power would come after being filled with the Spirit. It is, therefore, wrong to ask people to step out to be filled with power. They should come and be filled with the Holy Spirit. That is when they would receive power. This is because the power is of the Spirit.

Now, let's look at another verse: "Jesus returned to Galilee *in the power* of the Spirit, and news about him spread through the whole countryside" (Luke 4:14; emphasis added). Did you see that? Jesus was filled with the Spirit (Luke 4:1), and then he went into the desert. When he returned however, it was in the power of the Spirit. Filled with the Spirit, he went into the desert, but his return was in the Spirit's power. Take note that he was never filled with power. That's why he told his disciples that power would come when the Spirit comes upon them.

Many are filled with the Spirit with the evidence of tongues without manifesting any power. The reason for this is the absence of the desert experience. Between Jesus's being full of the Spirit and returning in the power of the Spirit was his experience in the desert (Luke 4:2–13). Jesus went into the desert to fast and pray, to seek the face of the Father. There, the enemy confronted him, and he overcame by the word. It was after this experience that he returned in the power of the Spirit.

This is the missing link today. Many are filled with the Holy Spirit but cannot demonstrate his power because they lack the desert experience. When the Holy Spirit comes on you, it is with power, but the desert experience is what stirs the power to manifestation. It is what fans it into flame. This was what Paul meant when he told Timothy to fan into flame the gift of God in him. To fan into flame, the minister needs to seek the Lord, in the closet like Jesus did in the desert.

Having shown that the Holy Spirit is not the power but that power comes after we receive the Holy Spirit and fan into flame the gift of God in us, the next question is, how do we keep the power? Without any form of circumlocution, the truth is that what it will take to keep the Holy Spirit in our lives is what it will take to keep the power. This is because the power is of the Spirit. In the absence of the Spirit, there will be no power. It is possible to have the Holy Spirit and yet not manifest power, not just by refusing to fan into flame the gift of God, but also by being ignorant and refusing to take the risk of acting out God's word. The chapter "Risk," in my first book, *A Future and a Hope* will open your eyes on this.

PROVISION

> Do not take any gold or silver or copper in your belts; take no bag for the journey, or extra tunic, or sandals or a staff; for the worker is worth his keep. (Matt 10:9–10)

The above speaks of the fourth operational P: *provision*. In these two verses, Jesus assured the disciples that their every need would be catered for. According to our Lord, they need not make any private arrangements for their upkeep, nor should they take clothes or extra luggage with them. Gold, silver, and copper speak of finance, the bag or extra luggage speaks of material acquisition, while the sandals or staff indicates social status. All these are unnecessary, as "the worker is worth his keep."

It is, therefore, disheartening to note that despite this divine assurance of provision, many still refuse the pull into ministry because they have not acquired a solid financial base. These are the ones who insist that they must first earn some money before entering into the ministry even though the Lord is asking them to move immediately. They insist that they don't want to suffer in the ministry, as such; they want to earn money to buy all the necessaries for a comfortable and successful ministry. These people are yet to fully come to terms with the instruction of Jesus: "Do not take along..."

"Do not take along" means do not take along! It is self-explanatory. It means, just go the way you have been sent, not even with your academic excellence! Jesus said, "As the father has sent me so send I you." When he was sent, it was with power (as we have already discussed). We also know from Scriptures that he did not go with truckloads of luggage or with a bank account piled up with hard currency. He went with nothing, yet he succeeded. He was able to feed five thousand, and four thousand on another occasion. He paid tax and was never hungry. He had so much money that he required a treasurer—Judas (John 12:4–6). I wish many ministers would seek God and his power and approval rather than material possession.

Today's church, it is sad to say, is filled with people who have abandoned their calling, their place, their purpose(s), and are chasing business deals. They no longer have time to pray or wait on the Lord. Those have now been delegated to their associate pastors or the prayer leaders. Their testimony is something like this: "When I first started out in the ministry, I used to pray at least four hours each day; I would fast twenty-one days at a stretch each month. Then anything I said came to pass. That was when I was paying the price. You young ones, you must pay the price too."

If you are such a minister, know that when your testimony is always about yesterday, it shows you have an empty today and you are condemned to a nonexistent tomorrow. Also note that while Saul was messing up, David was warming up. God is never in lack of men. That he picked you is a rare privilege—don't abuse it.

The instruction not to take anything along is not only clear but it still stands today. When God calls you, he does not abandon you nor does he leave you stranded. When he sends you on an *assignment*, he gives you a *consignment*; when he sends you on a *mission*, he gives you a *commission*. If he gives you a *vision*, he makes available the *provision*. This is what he means when he says "the worker is worth his keep."

Friend, no matter your fears, God is not going to abandon you. The quality of your life will not reduce as a result of your entrance into the ministry, so you need not pilfer ministry funds. The Master, Jesus himself, has made the provision. I worried too about these things, until the Lord made these Scriptures sink into my spirit:

"Therefore I tell you, do not worry about life, what you will eat or drink; or about your body, what you will wear. Is not life more important than food, and the body more important than clothes? Look at the birds of the air; they do not sow or reap or store away in barns, and yet your heavenly father feeds them. Are you not much more valuable than they? Who of you by worrying can add a single hour to his life?

> "And why do you worry about clothes? See how the lilies of the field grow. They do not labor or spin. Yet, I tell you that not even Solomon in all his splendor was dressed like one of these. If that is how God clothes the grass of the field, which is here today and tomorrow is thrown in the fire, will he not much more clothe you, O you of little faith? So do not worry saying, 'What shall we eat?' or 'What shall we drink?' or 'What shall we wear?' For the pagans run after all these things, and your heavily father knows that you need them. But seek first his kingdom and his righteousness, and all these things will be given you as well. Therefore do not worry about tomorrow, for tomorrow will worry about itself. Each day has enough trouble of its own." (Matt 6:25–34)

> God is not unjust; he will not forget your work and the love you have shown him as you have helped his people and continue to help them. (Heb 6:10)

The Lord showed me these Scriptures at a time when I was terribly scared of the consequences of entering into ministry. These Scriptures served to encourage me. I realized from them that he knows that I have need of physical wealth and material possessions, but he does not want me running after these things, so he made the provision to bring these things to me. The same applies to you.

Check the Scriptures; of all the men whom God used, not one of them lacked any good thing. Not one became the butt of jokes in their different societies. God was able to meet their needs. Do you know that the apostles whom Jesus asked to go without anything did not lack? It was recorded in Scriptures.

Then Jesus asked them, "When I sent you without purse, bag or sandals, did you lack anything?"

"Nothing," they answered. (Luke 22:35)

Jesus met their needs. They went with nothing yet they lacked nothing. If Jesus is the same yesterday, today, and forever, it means he will meet the needs of those he has called in these times just as he met those of the apostles.

Despite all these provisions, many ministers still live in penury. Others act as glorified beggars, using the privilege of the pulpit to milk the people. If you are such a minister, may you be delivered today! Amen.

Reasons for Lack

The reason why many ministers lack is either one or a combination of these three reasons: ignorance, greed, and wastefulness.

Ignorance

Ignorance of the provisions made available to them is one principal cause of lack amongst ministers. The popular verse, Hosea 4:6, "my people perish for lack of knowledge," is good enough cure. Such men should seek knowledge—knowledge concerning God's will for them as regards their provision. They also need to take very seriously this Scripture: "For you know the grace of our Lord Jesus Christ, that though he was rich, yet for your sakes he became poor, so that you through his poverty might become rich" (2 Cor 8:9).

Focusing on Wants

The second reason for lack is that most people pray for the meeting of their wants, not their needs. Scripture says my God shall supply all your *needs* (not all your *wants*). Friend, when those wants translate into needs, God will meet them, not before.

The distinction here between *want* and *need* is similar to the distinction between what is merely desirable and what is pertinent. Simply put, while wants can be ignored (i.e., you can go on without them), needs cannot be ignored—their absence creates serious problems. Economists teach that human wants are insatiable, but needs are satiable.

Waste

Wastefulness is another reason why so many ministers experience lack. They waste the resources of heaven in the name of abundance. God is against waste.

In the Old Testament, regarding the Passover, God instructed Israel that the meat from the lamb must be finished, there must be no leftovers. To avoid waste, he instructed that small families should come together and share one lamb. With respect to manna in the wilderness, God instructed that the people must pick only what they could eat, not more than what was necessary for a particular day.

The New Testament also contains events that show that God does not like waste under any guise. In the feeding of the five thousand and then the four thousand, the remains were gathered to avoid waste. In the first instance, twelve baskets remained and in the second, seven baskets remained. There was need for accountability to avoid waste.

Too many Christians waste the resources of heaven and then complain that God is unfaithful. When he gives, he expects you to be diligent, to be accountable, and not to be wasteful. Wastefulness is one reason why many ministries are in lack. If you don't have need for a thing, why buy it? Why enter into debt in order to acquire a piece of equipment? The resources of heaven have been given, but we must not waste them. We must not be slack in our use of it. The Bible says, "He becometh poor, that dealeth with a slack hand" (Prov 10:4 KJV).

God does not owe any man. He is not a debtor. He will rather give you more than you deserve, than owe you. As long as he called you, know that the provision is there already. His promises cannot be broken. Apostle Paul, after seeing the reality of the promises of God wrote:

> But as surely as God is faithful, our message to you is not "Yes" and "No." For the Son of God, Jesus Christ, who was preached among you by me and Silas and Timothy, was not "Yes" and "No," but in him it has always been "Yes." For no matter how many promises God has made, they are "Yes" in Christ. And so through him the "Amen" is spoken by us to the glory of God. (2 Cor 1:18–20)

One beautiful book on kingdom provision that I have no fear recommending to you is Kenneth Copeland's *Managing God's Mutual Funds—Yours and His*.

PEOPLE

> Whatever town or village you enter, search for some worthy person there and stay at his house until you leave. As you enter the home, give it your greeting. If the home is deserving let your peace rest on it; if it is not, let your peace return to you. If anyone will not welcome you or listen to your words, shake the dust off your feet when you leave that home or town. I tell you, the truth, it will be more bearable for Sodom and Gomorrah on the day of judgment than for that town. (Matt 10:11–15)

These five verses of Matthew 10 introduce us to the fifth operational P: *people*. Kindly, take a second look at these verses. We shall discuss this P from three perspectives: people as the targets of ministry, people who support ministers, and people who work alongside ministers.

People as Targets

A close look at Matthew 10:11–15 reveals that ministers are not just sent to people but that people constitute the target of the ministry. The ministers' focus should, therefore, be the people, with the sole aim of reaching and winning them over to the Master. Ministers should prayerfully devise plans and strategies on how to effectively reach and communicate their message to their congregation. They should have love and compassion for those they minister to.

But the situation on the ground is a far cry from this. Many ministers are wrongly focused. They have the wrong things as their target. Their aim is not to reach the people they have been sent to but to focus on themselves. Quite a number see ministry as an avenue to make money or purely as a source of livelihood. Some have as their target the building of empires from where their fame will spread across the globe. Others target gathering a crowd of hundreds of thousands so they can boast with it. In one word, the projection of "self" has become the aim of many.

Granted, no man does business with God and turns out a loser, but ministry is not for personal aggrandizement. God's target is to reach the people. The reason he pulled, prepared, and pushed you to a place with divine purpose, power, and provision is to reach the people. No wonder Scripture says:

> It was he who gave some to be apostles, some to be prophets, some to be evangelists, and some to

> be pastors and teachers, to prepare God's people for works of service, so that the body of Christ may be built up until we all [the minister and the people] reach unity in the faith and in the knowledge of the Son of God and become mature, attaining to the whole measure of the fullness of Christ. (Eph 4:11–13)

Beloved, the reason God called you is to prepare God's people (for works of service), not to build empires, not to amass wealth, and not to make a name for yourself. The people constitute the reason for your calling.

Going back to our text (Matt 10:11–15), the phrases "search for" and "if anyone will not welcome you" reveal that ministers must search out the people. They must go after them. They must find them. Of his own ministry, Jesus himself said, "The Son of Man is come to *seek* and to save that which was lost" (Luke 19:10; emphasis added). He came to seek them. He ran after them. It was so important to him that he had no time to search for an apartment where he could live, let alone build one. He was everywhere—looking for, searching for, and seeking the people. Today, a large number of those he called sit in big air-conditioned offices shaking their heads, tapping their feet, and admiring their latest ties. Instead of seeking the people, they wait for the people to come after them. To tell the truth, some ministers have not personally witnessed to anybody in the last five years, as they have more "pressing matters" to attend to.

Another sad development is that a lot of our churches have become "Christian centers," more like social and entertainment clubs. I say this because a good number of our pastors specialize in thrilling the crowd that comes to hear them. Many have little or no interpersonal contact (let alone relationship) with their members. I even heard a guest minister charge the pastor of the congregation to which he was invited to speak, "It is not your job to visit the people; send others there."

While I agree that it is not the sole responsibility of ministers to visit (others need to join them), and while I also do know and agree that ministers need time to seek the Lord's face, attend to their personal and family needs, and do other things, I believe that the absolute declaration that they have no business visiting the people is not true. I have seen church bulletins state (without any information on regular counseling times): "to see the pastor is strictly by appointment." For goodness sake, what about emergencies? This attitude is justified as ministerial ethics. But we do know that many saw Jesus without booking prior appointments: the centurion, the importunate widow, the woman with the issue of blood, and the rich young man. Jesus also visited the people: Mary and Martha, Zacchaeus, and others. Furthermore, the infallible, unchanging word of God charges every minister: "Be diligent to know the state of thy flocks, and look well to thy herds" (Prov 27:23 KJV).

How many ministers know the state of their flocks? Many know only the size and number. Many see their members as figures and nothing more. Ministers need to realize that people want to be seen and dealt with as persons, not as people. What I mean is that people want to be dealt with on an individual basis, not in large groupings. People want to be valued because they are humans, not for what they possess or can give. Jesus interacted with the rich and the poor during his time on earth. He had them in his trail throughout, and there is not a single mention of poor treatment of these people.

Today's church has also witnessed an increase in the dichotomy and distinction between the laity and the clergy. Many members find it difficult confiding in their pastors and church leaders. This is because time and again, many leaders have proven themselves inaccessible or have broken their confidence. A situation where a pastor turns into a topic for family discussion what had been told in confidence during counseling or uses the experiences of members to preach and teach or to admonish others who come for counseling is condemnable. Ministers should realize that whatever they see and hear in the course of ministry is privileged information. Such confidences should not be broken and such incidents should not necessarily become a mandatory consideration in the appointment of people into offices and positions in church.

People as Supporters

Apart from being the target or focus of ministry, people also perform another function in the life of ministers. Let's review verse 11 of Matthew 10: "Whatever town or village you enter, search for some worthy person there and stay at his house until you leave." From this Scripture, it is clear that the apostles were to be accommodated and cared for by the people they were sent to. The reason why Jesus had instructed the apostles to go on their divine assignment without bothering about their upkeep and survival is because their upkeep and survival had been divinely placed in the hands of the people they were to reach.

Paul, writing to the Corinthian church, discusses this issue extensively in chapter 9 of his first letter. While I suggest that you study this chapter, let's look at some of its salient provisions:

> Who serves as a soldier at his own expense? Who plants a vineyard and does not eat of its grapes? Who tends a flock and does not drink of its milk? ... If we have sown spiritual seed among you, is it too much if we reap a material harvest from you? ... Don't you know that those who work in the temple get their fruit from the temple, and those who serve at the altar share in what is offered on the altar? In the same way, the Lord has commanded that those who preach the gospel should receive their living from the gospel. (1 Cor 9:7, 11, 13, 14)

The point is this: the Lord has placed the material well-being of the minister in the hands of those he ministers to. God has divinely endowed the people with all it takes to make his ministers comfortable. This is to ensure that their work and labor in the ministry do not suffer as a result of lack. As the people bless the minister, the Lord blesses the people in return. This will not only ensure that the minister effectively labors in word and doctrine but that the people themselves do not lack. The propriety of this position is evident from this statement by our Lord:

> Anyone who receives a prophet because he is a prophet will receive a prophet's reward, and anyone who receives a righteous man because he is a righteous man will receive a righteous man's reward. And if anyone gives even a cup of cold water to one of these little ones because he is my

disciple, I tell you the truth, he will certainly not
lose his reward. (Matt 10:41-42)

To this end, people represent the connections, the opportunities, and the links that the minister requires to succeed. The minister, however, needs to search them out and reach them with the gospel. As he ministers the word to them, they, in turn, will minister to him materially. The experiences of Apostle Paul and how his needs were met further support the position being canvassed here.

> For even when I was in Thessalonica, you sent me aid again and again when I was in need. Not that I am looking for a gift, but I am looking for what may be credited to your account. I have received full payment and even more; I am amply supplied, now that I have received from Epaphroditus the gifts you sent. They are a fragrant offering, an acceptable sacrifice pleasing to God. (Phil 4:16-18)

Romans 16 contains a list of all who had in one way or the other assisted (or ministered to) Paul in his work in Rome. Let's take a snappy look at this list:

> I commend to you our sister Phoebe, a servant of the church in Cenchrea. I ask you to receive her in the Lord in a way worthy of the saints and to give her any help she may need from you, for she has been a great help to many people, including me. Greet Priscilla and Aquila, my fellow workers in Christ Jesus. They risked their lives for me. Not only I but all the churches of the Gentiles are grateful to them. . . . Greet Andronicus and Junias, my relatives who have been in prison

> with me. . . . Greet Urbanus, our fellow worker in Christ, and my dear friend Stachys. . . . Greet Tryphena and Tryphosa, those women who work hard in the Lord. Greet my friend Rufus, chosen in the Lord, and his mother, who has been a mother to me, too. . . . Timothy, my fellow worker, sends his greetings to you as do Lucius, Jason and Sosipater, my relatives. I, Tertius, who wrote down this letter, greet you in the Lord. Gaius, whose hospitality I and the whole church here enjoy, sends you his greetings. Erastus, who is the city's director of public works, and our brother Quartus send you their greetings.

What a list! Paul had help in different ways and from different people. Help, not just for ministry purposes, but also for his personal needs. The importance of people in ministry cannot be overemphasized.

The statement of Elkanah O. Oluwagbesan, district overseer of the Otta District of the Foursquare Gospel Church in Nigeria, at the Ajebo 2000 International Ministers and Leaders Conference is not only insightful but worth reproducing here: "Foursquare Movement was founded and established on laity potentials. To keep the Movement flying requires mobilization and maximization of laity potentials. The greatest blessing to a church is that of active laity who are assets to the pastor." I make bold to say that the New Testament church (not just the Foursquare Movement) was founded and established on laity potentials. The growth of the church and her impact has been stunted because of overemphasis and overexpectation from the clergy.

Pastors and church leaders should not only take note but also allow the last limb of Oluwagbesan's quotation to sink into them: "The greatest blessing to a church is that of active laity who are assets to the pastor." Sadly, many pastors are scared of the laity. Many would rather dine with the devil and drink of his poison than give opportunities to the laity. The greatest blessing to a church is not the church accounts or landed property but the laity.

But then, we must note that Jesus did not ask the apostles to bargain or plead with the people (see verse 14). They were not to *doctor* or adulterate their message. They were instructed to depart if they were not welcomed. They were not to bend the message in order to become accepted.

To our dismay, today's church is filled with people preaching doctored messages because they want the approval and support of the crowd. Our preachers and teachers have adjusted their messages, shifted a little from the divine mandate that caused God to pull them, switched from the places they were originally sent to, so they can "belong" and be referred to as "big time" or successful preachers. This generation has witnessed a rise in the surge of ministers of men and a sharp decline in the availability of "ministers of God." Many abandoned their calling a long time ago. Today some are working for their bishops, their general overseers, their sponsors, and so on. They are content with being identified with a big name in the ministry. Heaven is bleeding for such men because they have no business in the places where they are currently positioned. Time and again, the Holy Spirit has nudged them to move into the fullness of their calling, but they have refused; they value man's approval more than God's. But the Scripture is clear:

"And he said unto them, 'Ye are they which justify yourselves before men; but God knoweth your hearts: for that which is highly esteemed among men is abomination in the sight of God' " (Luke 16:15 KJV).

Ministry People

The last and final category under which we shall discuss *people* consists of people who work with the minister. Simply put, these are people whom the minister needs to involve and or be involved with, in the course of ministry operations. This category is different from the two earlier categories because the people in this category are also ministers and their relationship with the minister is primarily in the sphere of ministry itself.

The importance of ministry people stems from the fact that there is no account of solo ministry in the Scriptures. Moses had Aaron, Joshua, and Hur. Elijah had Elisha who in turn had Gehazi, Jeremiah had Baruch, David his mighty men, and Jesus the twelve. Also, in sending out the seventy, Jesus sent them two by two.

It is pertinent to mention here that how the minister handles his relationship with this class of persons can make or break him. For ease of communication and presentation of material, we shall discuss people in the ministry under the following subheads: mentors, protégés, peers, and helpers.

Mentors

There is today a lopsided understanding of who a mentor is and what mentoring is all about. Many people (within and outside Christendom) lay claim to being mentors or to have mentored people when, in actual fact, they have done no such thing. The craze about mentorship particularly in the Nigerian church (and society) is rooted in the desire to be called "papa" or be tagged the "spiritual father" of someone, or for the supposed mentor to be able to say publicly, " That is my boy in the ministry," or, "I brought him up."

While I personally do not have anything against calling anyone "papa" or "son" (Scriptures also do not condemn it, for Paul in his epistles often referred to Timothy as his son in the faith), a good number of "ministry greats," as I call them, act more like models towards a large percentage of the upcoming generation of ministers than like mentors. (I write this with great fear and humility, knowing that I have benefited from the teachings of these great men in live services and through their books and tapes. So it is with all due respect that I, an "unknown," as it were, writes this.) Knowing who a mentor is will help us understand the difference between a mentor and a model. Suffice it to say however, that a model is a point of reference or a standard that inspires a person, with or without personal contact.

In chapter 6 of her beautiful book, *The Voice of God*, the great woman of God, Cindy Jacobs, discusses extensively the concept of mentorship and the challenges that go along with it. She cites and quotes Robert Clinton's definition of mentoring and his views on who a mentor is, as contained in Clinton's book, *The Making of a Leader*. Clinton defines mentoring as follows:

> Mentoring refers to the process where a person with a serving, giving, encouraging attitude, the mentor, sees leadership potential in a still-to-be developed person, the protégé, and is able to

promote or otherwise significantly influence the protégé along in the realization of potential.

On who a mentor is, Clinton writes,

> A mentor is someone who helps a protégé in some very practical ways; by risking his or her own reputation in backing the protégé; by giving timely advice that encourages the protégé, by bridging between the protégé and needed resources; by modeling and setting expectations that challenge the protégé; by giving tracts, letters, books or other literary information that open perspectives for the protégé, by giving financially, sometimes sacrificially, to further the protégé's ministry, by co-ministering in order to increase the credibility, status and prestige of the protégé; and by having the freedom to allow and even promote the protégé beyond the mentor's own level of leadership. (p. 114–115)

I concur with Clinton's definition and explanation of mentorship and recommend that you go through it again so that you can follow closely when we begin to examine it.

You will notice that mentoring, according to Clinton, is a *process*. It is not a one-time thing. The process of mentoring is a long and laborious one. The protégé may be a slow learner or there may be many truths that require a long time for effective communication and grasp. Thus, an elder in the ministry who has had the privilege of counseling or praying for and with a younger minister, once or twice, is not (necessarily) a mentor to that younger minister.

A close look at Clinton's definition also shows that the mentor "sees leadership potential in a still-to-be-developed person," not leadership qualities or abilities in an already developed person. Many people claiming to be mentors do not desire (let alone attempt) to discover leadership potential in still-to-be-developed persons, but are actually looking for those already developed. Thus, by Clinton's definition, they are not mentors.

A third thing we must observe in Clinton's definition is that, upon the discovery of leadership potential, the mentor begins to promote or significantly influence the protégé "in the realization of potential." Sadly, today's mentors do little or nothing about promoting the protégé and their supposed influence does not extend beyond their lips. Those who claim to do so, do it, not in the terms contained in Clinton's definition: "along in the realization of potential," but in the realization of the work, goals, and objectives of their own (the mentor's own) ministry. However, I must be quick to add that there are exceptions.

Clinton goes on to give a word-picture of the functions of a mentor: giving timely advice, encouragement, providing or assisting in the provision of resources, being a role model, providing literature (this could include audio and video tapes), co-ministering with the protégé and all such things that will not only promote the protégé but would increase his credibility and enhance his effectiveness in ministry.

A look at the foregoing functions shows that mentoring encompasses and extends beyond modeling. Modeling involves being a standard or point of reference and may sometimes extend to helping in the setting of standards. Mentoring involves these and even more. The truth is that mentoring is no easy task. It involves the complete communication and transfer of all organized knowledge, skills, and experience possessed by the mentor into the protégé. It is more or less a reproduction of the mentor in a protégé. For this to be effectively done, the mentor and the protégé should constantly have time together or at least, the protégé should have unrestricted access to the mentor.

Disappointments are a sure feature in the mentoring process. Hence, mentors should never expect protégés to always be up and doing. Some may be slow in their grasp of the truths and skills being conveyed, others may even, after they begin to grasp concepts, make silly mistakes. Protégés, at this point, need encouragement (not pampering) and firm but loving discipline (not a severance of the relationship). Once again, mentoring is no easy task. Jesus himself, in spite of the multitudes that followed him, could only mentor twelve persons.

To this end, I humbly submit that no mentoring takes place without a functional interpersonal relationship between the mentor and the protégé. The idea of long-distance mentoring via books and tapes alone, without any existing relationship (and communication) between the mentor and the protégé makes a mockery of the entire concept of mentoring and is, to say the least, fallacious.

The book, *Stories for the Heart*, a collection of articles and short stories, put together by Alice Gray, contains an article on mentoring by Chip McGregor. The article centers on how Sherwood Anderson, the great author, mentored the likes of Ernest Hemmingway, William Faulkner, Thomas Wolfe, and John Steinbeck. Anderson himself had sat under the influence of the great Theodore Dreiser and had spent quality time with Carl Sandburg. McGregor concludes his inspiring article this way:

> I find this pattern instructive. Not only does it mirror my own experience, it also illustrates what I have found to be a fundamental human experience—that the greatest means of impacting the future is to build into another person's life. This process is called mentoring. (p. 106)

I cannot help but agree with McGregor. If mentoring does not affect the future through the protégé, into whom the mentor has "sown" himself, then the effort is not worth it.

Protégés

Simply put, a protégé is the pupil, student, or understudy of the mentor. A protégé learns from the mentor. He must not only be willing to learn from the mentor, but must also be ready to submit to his authority and oversight. Let me also add that, from my little experience and observation, most protégés have more than one mentor, usually a different mentor for a different phase of their lives.

Protégés must be willing to grow and be ready to take initiative on their own. They must not confine themselves to being protégés for life. In fact, they should aspire to become mentors, too. It is, however, sad to say that most people want to remain protégés for life. They want to be perpetually tutored. In some cases, mentors don't want to let go of their protégés. This is sad. On the other hand, after being mentored, many bite the fingers that fed them and those who mentored them end up refusing to mentor others. It is, therefore, necessary to say here that protégés should not have unrealistic expectations or make ridiculous demands from their mentors. They should learn to be appreciative of their mentors.

Mentor-Protégé Relationships in Scriptures

There are countless examples of mentor-protégé relationships in Scriptures. We shall look at some of them and see what lessons can be learned from them.

Moses and Joshua

> The LORD would speak to Moses face to face, as a man speaks with his friend. Then Moses would return to the camp, but his young aide Joshua son of Nun did not leave the tent. (Exod 33:11)

The description of Joshua as the young aide of Moses speaks of Joshua as a protégé to Moses and the latter as his mentor. It is well to mention too that although Moses mentored Joshua and at the end of his ministry passed on the leadership baton to him, Joshua's heart was set after God, to know him for himself. Hence, Joshua did not leave the tent of meeting even after Moses's return to the camp.

What is the point? Protégés should, while understudying their mentors, seek and strive to know God for themselves, and mentors should not only take time to teach and show their protégés the secrets of their success but should as of first importance point them to God. This was what Moses illustrated by taking Joshua along to the tent of meeting.

Eli and Samuel

> Then Elkanah went home to Ramah, but the boy ministered *before* the LORD *under* Eli the priest. (1 Sam 2:11; emphasis added)

The relationship between Eli, the priest, and Samuel, was also that of mentor-protégé. The Scripture above says Samuel ministered *under* Eli the priest. This illustrates the fact that, when Samuel understudied Eli, he accepted the priest as his mentor. Samuel was never rebellious, nor did he plot to unseat the old priest like many protégés are apt to do today. He was under, subject to, and accountable to Eli.

Notice also that, like Joshua, Samuel sought to know God experientially, hence he ministered "before the Lord," not before Eli. This is unlike what we find today. Most protégés minister before their mentors (not before the Lord) in order to gain approval. Many a mentor would seem not only to have encouraged this untoward trend but also actively endorsed and rewarded it.

It is also important to note that according to the account of Scriptures, Samuel had a place of meeting with the Lord.

> The boy Samuel ministered before the LORD under Eli. In those days the word of the LORD was rare; there were not many visions. One night Eli, whose eyes were becoming so weak that he could barely see, was lying down *in his usual place.* The lamp of God had not yet gone out, and *Samuel was lying down in the temple of the Lord, where the ark of God was.* (1 Sam 3:1–3; emphasis added)

This account describes Eli's place as "his usual place" meaning the old priest was always there; it was his custom to be there. But the Bible says that Samuel was lying down in the temple, where the ark was kept. The ark signifies the presence of God—that was where Samuel was, but Eli was not there. He was in his usual place where the presence of God was absent.

What lesson can we learn? Protégés should seek and cultivate a relationship with the Lord on a personal note. This would ensure that if the mentor loses touch with the Master, the protégé could still be in touch. We may also add that while protégés need mentors to learn from, their ministry and heart's cry should be to know God and be anointed by him and him alone.

Apollos, Priscilla, and Aquila

The story of Priscilla and Aquila, and their contact and subsequent relationship with Apollos, is a New Testament example of mentor-protégé relationships.

> Meanwhile a Jew named Apollos, a native of Alexandria, came to Ephesus. He was a learned man, with a thorough knowledge of the Scriptures. He had been instructed in the way of the Lord, and he spoke with great fervor and taught about Jesus accurately, though he knew only the baptism of John. He began to speak boldly in the synagogue. When Priscilla and Aquila heard him, they invited him to their home and explained to him the way of God more adequately. (Acts 18:24–26)

Apollos was not only educated by the standards of his day, he was also described as having a thorough knowledge of Scriptures and more than that, he had been instructed in the way of the Lord. In other words, Apollos was a balanced individual—a rare combination of the matchless grace of God and the thoroughbred academic.

Today, most ministers are not balanced. Those who are spiritually sound are academically and socially deficient, while those who are academically and socially sound are spiritually deficient. Many even lack a thorough knowledge of Scriptures and proper instruction in the way of the Lord.

Despite this seeming balance, Apollos had one problem—he knew only of the baptism of John. Worthy of note, however, is that he submitted himself to the teachings (mentoring) of Priscilla and Aquila and so made up what he lacked.

Here lies the difference between Apollos and our generation of ministers. We are anointed, worded, and "revved" up with great zeal and fervor, but like Apollos, we know only the "baptism of John." This means that we have yet to know the deep mysteries of the kingdom, mysteries encountered and discovered by the workings of the Holy Spirit.

However, unlike Apollos, who submitted to the teaching of Priscilla and Aquila, many of us are not ready to submit to, or hear from anybody. Apollos with all his reputation submitted himself to Priscilla and Aquila, as they explained the way of God more adequately to him. Note that Scripture says "more adequately" and not "accurately." This implies that Apollos had never gone wrong but he needed to be taught God's word deeply and extensively (not exhaustively because insights to the word of God are inexhaustible). I have seen and heard of many who left their churches and denominations because they have a "unique calling," and as such, need no mentoring or better still, cannot be mentored by anyone since they are the pioneers of their calling. Some are waiting to meet the men of God with global repute for mentoring, as those around them have nothing to offer. I pity such people. I have not said that the Lord cannot ask you to leave a place and begin elsewhere or on your own, but the way and manner in which many have left scares me stiff. Besides, I know God does not encourage confusion and strife.

A second thing we must note from the story of Apollos is expressed in these words: "When Priscilla and Aquila heard him, they invited him to their home." Apollos did not go to them; they came for him. Priscilla and Aquila went for Apollos because they knew they had something to offer. This is what many seniors and ministry greats of today are not willing to do. No one is taking interest in today's young and up-coming ministers who certainly will be the generals of tomorrow. While most Apolloses of today are scared of the Priscillas and Aquilas, most Priscillas and Aquilas believe that the Apolloses should run after them if they are serious. Both camps are plagued by the fear of rejection from each other. In some cases, interest would be taken if the Apolloses would become a part of the ministry of the Priscillas and Aquilas and remain there. In others, the Aquila and Priscillas, just to increase the list of protégés, extend invitations when they do not have anything to really offer.

The relationship between Paul and Timothy, and Paul and Titus are other examples of New Testament mentor-protégé relations. Paul's letters to these men are not only a must for ministers of this age but are model examples of what mentor-protégé relationships should look like.

Peers

> In the church at Antioch there were prophets and teachers. Barnabas, Simeon called Niger, Lucius of Cyrene, Manaen (who had been brought up with Herod the tetrarch) and Saul. While they were worshipping the Lord and fasting, the Holy Spirit said, "Set apart for me Barnabas and Saul for the work to which I have called them." So after they had fasted and prayed, they placed their hands on them and sent them off. (Acts 13:1–3)

All the men mentioned in verse 1 were peers, not in age, academics, or achievements, but in ministry. They related as equals, as prophets and teachers. *Peers*, as regards the context of our discourse, refers strictly to ministry peers (not childhood friends or peers in any other respect).

Peers in ministry may or may not have the same calling, may or may not have been sent to the same place jointly or severally, but the distinguishing factor is that one is not a mentor or protégé to the other. Peers relate with one another on the same level even though the dimensions and outlook of their ministries may differ.

From the passage under consideration, we also discover that Barnabas and Paul were ministry peers. They were given a joint assignment. Their relationship as recorded in chapters 13–15 of the Acts of the Apostles also illustrates this point. Let's quickly take an illustration from Acts 13:46–47: "Then Paul and Barnabas answered them boldly: 'We had to speak the word of God to you first; since you reject it and do not consider yourselves worthy of eternal life, we now turn to the Gentiles. For this is what the Lord has commanded us." Note the use of the plural pronoun, "we." They were sent jointly; it was not as if one was hired or was an understudy to the other. In the events recorded through chapters 13–15, they saw themselves as peers and contemporaries. Paul did not issue an instruction, as it were, to Barnabas, nor did Barnabas do the same. Theirs was a relationship governed by mutual agreement and the leading of the Holy Spirit. When they parted, there was no record of one blessing the other or seeking his permission, as would occur in a relationship between mentors and protégés.

Another example of peers in Scripture is seen in the relationship between Daniel, Shadrach, Meshach, and Abednego. These men, according to the account in Daniel 1 were peers. This view is further supported by the fact that, in chapter 2, when Daniel was confronted with the challenge of searching out and interpreting Nebuchadnezzar's dream, he went to Shadrach, Meshach and Abednego, and all four joined hands and prayed, and that same night the mystery of the King's dream was revealed to Daniel (Dan 2:17–19).

Helpers

Helpers, like peers, differ from protégés because they do not have a mentoring relationship with the minister. Helpers work closely with ministers but as fellow ministers, not as protégés or peers. The distinction between the helper and a peer is that, while peers need not necessarily work (in the same organization) with the minister, the helper must of necessity work with the minister. Assistants or helpers are themselves in ministry, but their calling is to assist in the fulfillment of the "main" minister's God-given calling.

The ministry of helpers is what has been referred to as the "armor-bearing" ministry. A biblical example of this kind of relationship is that which existed between Moses and Aaron before the latter was ordained a priest.

Aaron was not Moses's protégé (as was Joshua), neither was he Moses's peer. He was an assistant or helper to Moses. Aaron, before his ordination as a priest, received no special commission from God. His assignment was to walk and work with Moses as the latter strove to fulfill his divine mandate.

In the New Testament, both Jesus and the apostle Paul had helpers in their ministries. Jesus had people (outside the twelve) who attended to his needs. By their ministration, they assisted or helped in his work to bring ease to it. This is the primary function of helpers. Paul had Tertius, Pablus, and a host of others listed in Romans 16, who were helpers in his ministry. They were not his protégés, as were Titus and Timothy.

A contemporary example of a helper-minister is David Abioye, second bishop of the Living Faith Church (also known as Winners' Chapel). Abioye has repeatedly (and particularly in his book, *Stewardship: The Pathway to Honor*) said that his primary calling is to support and see to the success of the ministry of David Oyedepo, the founding bishop. In that book, Abioye repeatedly refers to Oyedepo as "my master."

Perhaps, no other minister in Nigeria can tell the importance and joy of having helpers more than Francis Wale Oke, presiding bishop of the Christ Life Church and president of the Sword of the Spirit Ministries. At the inauguration of Christ Life Church on February 11, 1989, all the elders of the nondenominational fellowship being led by Oke backed out, leaving only his wife and two other persons. One of them, Oriname Oyonnude Kure, now bishop of the Evidence of the Gospel Church, Benin City, looked at Oke with a rugged and unshaken determination and said, "Sir, whatever you ask us to do, I am with you." To this day, Francis Wale Oke's heart still blesses Oyonnude Kure. No wonder Francis Wale Oke was a key player at the ordination of Kure as bishop on Saturday, February 9, 2002.

Ministry helpers may not be popular ministers. In most cases, they are not even seen as ministers. This is because many of them keep secular jobs or may function as personal assistants, administrative officers, media and publicity chiefs, interpreters, and so on. Their primary task is to assist and provide physical help (and sometimes, material help), for the main ministers, thus easing the burden of the ministry.

It is disheartening, therefore, to note that many heads of ministries or "main" ministers treat shabbily or with little respect, the men who function as helpers. The situation is worse where these helpers do not keep secular jobs but are full-time workers in the ministries or organizations of these main ministers. If in a church-based ministry, the helper may be serving as an associate pastor or head of department. Most times where this is the case, such helpers hardly ever get any opportunity to preach, sometimes throughout a whole year. There is always a guest minister when the main minister is not around, or one is quickly arranged, if the main minister is traveling on emergency. This is one of the major reasons behind the many break-ups in our churches.

Main ministers should realize that God also called these helpers who serve as associates and they would sometimes desire to preach and teach (or function in whatever calling they have). They should create room to have them minister, not just during weekday services but also on Sundays and during special programs. Main ministers should also take time out to publicly appreciate the efforts and labors of their helpers. The Bible says in Proverbs, "The crucible for the silver and the furnace for the gold, but a man is tested by the praise he receives" (Prov 27:21).

Some helpers, by their excesses, have aided the seeming distrust and lack of confidence existing between main ministers and helpers. Many deliberately (although a few unconsciously) incite the people against the main ministers by sowing discord in an attempt to steal (yes, steal!) the flock away from the main ministers to themselves. Such men should be careful—he who pelts another with pebbles asks for rocks in return.

The Dynamic Nature of Relationships

Having discussed the four categories of people encountered in ministry, it is well to say here that the categories are not static. By this, I mean that no one is permanently confined to any of these categories. There is room for growth, development, and change. Scriptures tell us in 2 Corinthians 3:18 that we are transformed from glory to glory (one level to the next, one phase to another) by the Spirit of the Lord. Thus, protégés grow to become mentors to those coming behind them. Some even grow to become peers with their erstwhile mentors, and in very rare cases, they may even end up mentoring those who previously mentored them.

In her book, *The Voice of God*, Cindy Jacobs gives what I consider to be a modern-day example of a situation where roles changed and grew. She shares the experience of her local church, which was started in 1986 as the Mountain Shadows Christian Church by Bob Stennett, who served as pastor for several years. In 1992, the Lord showed Bob that he was to allow Dutch Sheets to become the senior pastor while he became the associate pastor. And since then, Dutch Sheets has been pastoring the church. Did I hear you say, "Not in a Nigerian church!"? In Nigeria, such an event would be viewed as an abuse of the anointing on the life of the senior or founding pastor. Nevertheless, the Lord does call the first to be last and the last to be first.

As for peers, those who start out as peers do not always remain peers. While the ministry of one may grow, that of the other may be stagnated. The reasons behind such differences in ministries are many and varied, but they are not very much different from the issues discussed in this book. In Daniel 1, we find that Daniel, Shadrach, Meshach and Abednego started out as peers, but Daniel was later uplifted to a higher position. It is noteworthy that Daniel used his new position to also secure upliftment for his friends (Dan 2:48–49).

Helpers may, in the course of helping, receive a divine mandate from God as regards a specific task of ministry. A biblical example is Aaron, who began as a helper to Moses but finally ended up being chosen by God to pioneer and head the priesthood in Israel. A contemporary example in this regard is the highly revered but unassuming Enoch Adejare Adeboye (better known as Pastor Adeboye), who, before he became general overseer of the Redeemed

Christian Church of God, was the interpreter to the late founder and pioneer general overseer, Josiah Oluwafemi Akindayomi.

Friend, what I want to pass across is this: your current position is not your final position. Therefore, make it your business to faithfully carry out whatever assignment you have been given. And if you are privileged to head a ministry, be open and flexible enough to recognize, accept, and even encourage your helpers (just as the church in Ephesus did for Apollos when he was to leave for Achaia in Acts 18:27–28) when God hands over divine mandate to them. We are not in competition with one another. Our enemy is Satan and his demons.

PRECAUTION

> I am sending you out like sheep among wolves. Therefore be as shrewd as snakes and as innocent as doves. (Matt 10:16)

The above verse deals with the last and final operational P. In sending the disciples out into the villages and towns of Israel, Jesus gave them one precautionary measure to observe. This precaution is expressed in verse 16, and we shall quickly examine the import of this precaution to us modern-day disciples whom he has sent out.

Even though the disciples needed the people (for the different purposes which we have examined under the last P) and were to accept whatever hospitality they were offered, they were to be cautious in their dealings with the people, the reason being that some people would be wolves in sheep's clothing, Satan dressed up as a saint, fiends instead of friends. Thus, Jesus cautioned that the disciples were to be as shrewd as snakes but innocent as doves.

Apostle Paul had a dose of men who appeared to be friends when, in fact, they were fiends. In 2 Timothy 1:15 and 4:9–18, the apostle not only mentioned the names of some of these men, but he also charged Timothy, his protégé to be careful of them.

> You know that everyone in the province of Asia has deserted me, including Phygelus and Hermogenes. . . . Do your best to come to me quickly, for Demas, because he loved this world, has deserted me and has gone to Thessalonica. . . . Alexander the metal worker did me a great deal of harm. The Lord will repay him for what he has done. You too should be on your guard against him, because he strongly opposed our message. At my first defense, no one came to my support, but everyone deserted me. May it not be held against them? (2 Tim 1:15, 4:9–10, 14–16)

Phygelus, Hermogenes, Demas, and Alexander must have been men Paul relied upon, but they disappointed him. Then, Paul had the shock of his life when all the brethren abandoned him during his trial.

The point is that while the importance of people cannot be overemphasized, particularly in the areas we have discussed (as target, support, and cohort), ministers still need to take precaution in dealing with them. Every minister must be careful of people: the people he works with, the congregation he ministers to, or the crowd that follows him. Rehoboam, son of Solomon, failed because he did not take precautionary measures in his relationships. Samson, the deliverer of Israel, failed for the same reason. Today, many have also failed for this same reason.

Ministers should realize that they need to be careful not only in dealing with the unsaved but also be more careful in dealing with believers—those in the family of God with seeming godly counsel. Jesus told us, "A man's enemies will be the members of his own household (Matt 10:36)." And do you know that the members of Jesus's household, his own brothers and sisters, were the first to declare him insane, before the Pharisees and teachers of the law did?

> When his family heard about this, they went to take charge of him, for they said, "He is out of his mind." And the teachers of the law who came down from Jerusalem said, "He is possessed by Beelzebub! By the prince of demons he is driving out demons." (Mark 3:21–22)

His kith and kin called him insane, and then the people declared him a demoniac. Friend, let's not forget that we've been sent as sheep among wolves; we ought to be cautious. Though as ministers, we need people for the reasons discussed above, we need to be on our guard. Many ministries have been wrecked and destroyed, visions blurred, hopes shattered, dreams fizzled out, all because the men did not observe the precaution Jesus gave. The neighbor's prayer, "God save us from our friends, for we know who our enemies are" is apt here.

Jesus's declaration that a man's enemies will be the members of his own household makes it imperative that we examine the role of the minister's spouse (the number one person with whom the minister relates in his household) in his ministry. Otherwise, our discourse on the precaution Jesus gave will be incomplete.

The position of Scriptures with respect to marriage holds true for all Christians whether they be ministers or not. In a nutshell, Scriptures admonish that Christians love their spouses and live with them according to scriptural standards. Those who have focused on family life teachings from the Bible have written so much on this. I do not, therefore, intend to dwell so much on this. But one issue demands careful examination: to what extent should the minister's spouse influence or be involved in his or her ministry?

No one could have put it better than Tunde Bakare, the daring pastor of the Latter Rain Assembly, in Lagos, Nigeria, whose prophetic ministry has had great impact on the Nigerian nation. When asked why he's de-emphasized his wife in the ministry unlike other ministers of God, Tunde Bakare was quoted to have responded as follows in the Saturday, July 1, 2000, edition of the *Guardian*:

> I have never de-emphasised my wife in this ministry. She functions. Every Sunday, when you come here, you'll find her holding the microphone. But you see the idea of co-pastor is not even scriptural. Any animal with two heads is a monster. If my wife is in pastoral office, she would fulfill that office. But first and foremost, she is my wife. She is pastor's wife. And she is doing her best to support the vision God has given me. My wife will not tell you that she heard the call when God called me. So she's studying her own call. And when she finds out what that call is, we will release her into it. But administrative-

ly, she is helping with what I am doing and she's part of what I am doing, and she's contributing her quota. She's not been de-emphasised in any form but she's not my co-pastor. She might be a pastor in her own right, or in any of the ministries that God would give her. She's my strongest prayer warrior and intercessor, mother of my lovely five children and a good one at that, and a wife I appreciate tremendously. But she's not the set man at the Latter Rain Assembly. *I listen to her counsel when she talks to me, but I take instructions from God.* That's the situation here. She's not de-emphasized. We just don't want to do what every other person does and says, when a man is called, the wife is automatically called. If it was so, Moses and Zipporah should have been set over Israel. But you remember, like I saw in the film *Moses*, Zipporah said, "When he was looking for his God, I found him; when he found his God, I lost him." When Moses stepped out to go do that which God gave him, Zipporah did not go. It took a while before Jethro, her father, brought her back to Moses in the wilderness. So the idea of co-pastor is not scriptural. I am not saying that some of the pastors' wives are not called, what I am saying is, they should prove that call. It's not automatic that because their husbands are pastors, they should be pastoresses. That's the problem you have in Nigeria when you have an unconstitutional office of the First Lady. Very Unconstitutional. Every kobo spent from the treasury is stolen because that office is not a constitutional provision. The president's wife is the president's wife. She should manage his bedroom and the affairs of their family. They should stop meddling as interlopers with the affairs of this nation. So it should be in the church. (emphasis added)

Bakare's answer is both impressive and instructive and would very well serve as study material on the place of the minister's spouse in the ministry. Of particular note are the emphasized words in Bakare's answer, which are to the effect that the minister's spouse, who as a result of the intimate relationship they share would inevitably be the minister's primary (if not most influential) counselor, should never be allowed to replace the Holy Spirit and his instructions.

Another useful material in this regard would be Oretha Hagin's (Kenneth E. Hagin's wife) book, *The Price Is Not Greater Than God's Grace*. Oretha's book is highly recommended as it treats these issues from an experiential perspective.

Finally, let's close our discourse on precaution by looking closely at the danger of unnecessary hobnobbing with the crowd and not heeding the Master's caution, as pictured in this poem, which I wrote on April 5, 2001:

The Crowd

What lovely sight to behold!
The security they offer
Nothing to shelve or be sold
Nothing to shame or suffer
The multitude of voices heard
Loud claps and cheers
The oohs and aahs
The laughter and tears
But the mystique of the crowd—

Consistently inconsistent.
Here today and there tomorrow
Crown him now to crucify him later
Praises and boos intertwined
Expectations unknowingly certain
Going wherever the wind blows
What folly to rely on such rating
Let this realization hit you:
The crowd is never with you
Their support, a mirage
You're on stage; they are not
Your fall does them no harm
They're secured from falling
Let this realization hit you:
Crown him now to crucify him later

3

The Storm-Oriented Ps

Our discourse shall now center on what I have called the storm-oriented Ps. I realize that the term *storm-oriented* presupposes danger, trouble, and crises. No one wants these things, particularly in our feel good, live great world of today. Believers are also caught in the frenzy of this trend. I know from Scriptures that God promised to be with us as he takes us through life, but I know of no place where it is written that the journey through life will be stress-free, trouble-free, or sweat-free.

> But now, this is what the LORD says—
> he who created you, O Jacob,
> he who formed you, O Israel:
> "Fear not, for I have redeemed you;
> I have summoned you by name; you are mine.
> When you pass through the waters,
> I will be with you;
> and when you pass through the rivers,
> they will not sweep over you.
> When you walk through the fire,
> you will not be burned;
> the flames will not set you ablaze.
> For I am the LORD, your God,
> the Holy One of Israel, your Savior;
> I give Egypt for your ransom,

> Cush and Seba in your stead.
> Since you are precious and honored in my sight,
> and because I love you,
> I will give men in exchange for you,
> and people in exchange for your life. (Isa 43:1–4)

God is with us all the way. When we go through the waters, through the fire, through the storms, he is there with us.

Beloved, as long as we are alive, we will go through storms. Being a minister does not rule you out. But as ministers, the promise of divine presence also applies to us.

The storm-oriented Ps are in verses 17–31 of our Matthew text:

> "Be on your guard against men; they will hand you over to the local councils and flog you in their synagogues. On my account you will be brought before governors and kings as witnesses to them and to the Gentiles. But when they arrest you, do not worry about what to say or how to say it. At that time you will be given what to say, for it will not be you speaking, but the Spirit of your Father speaking through you.
>
> "Brother will betray brother to death, and a father his child; children will rebel against their parents and have them put to death. All men will hate you because of me, but he who stands firm to the end will be saved. When you are persecuted in one place, flee to another. I tell you the truth, you will not finish going through the cities of Israel before the Son of Man comes.
>
> "A student is not above his teacher, nor a servant above his master. It is enough for the stu-

dent to be like his teacher, and the servant like his master. If the head of a house has been called Beelzebub, how much more the members of his household?

"So do not be afraid of them. There is nothing concealed that will not be disclosed, or hidden that will not be made known. What I tell you in the dark, speak in the daylight; what is whispered in your ear, proclaim from the roofs. Do not be afraid of those who kill the body but cannot kill the soul. Rather, be afraid of the One who can destroy both soul and body in hell. Are not two sparrows sold for a penny? Yet, not one of them will fall to the ground apart from the will of your Father. And even the very hairs of your head are all numbered. So don't be afraid; you are worth more than many sparrows.

PERSECUTION

The first of the storm-oriented Ps is contained in verses 17–18: "Be on your guard against men; they will hand you over to the local councils and flog you in their synagogues. On my account you will be brought before governors and kings as witnesses to them and to the Gentiles." These are strong but clear words that require no special skill to tell their meaning. Jesus told the apostles (and by extension, ministers of today), that persecution must come their way. We shall be arrested, beaten, and disgraced because of his gospel. We cannot escape it. It must come. Prayers and fasting, tongues, emptying bottles of olive oil, and the use of handkerchiefs will not stop it. Persecution is a mandatory component of ministry. Why? He tells us: "A student is not above his teacher, nor a servant above his master. It is enough for the student to be like his teacher and the servant like his master. If the head of a house has been called Beelzebub, how much more the members of his household?" (Matt 10:24–25). The import of Jesus's statement is that since he was persecuted, his followers—those called—must be persecuted.

Remember, he declared to the disciples, "As the Father has sent me, I am sending you" (John 20:21). The Father sent him, yet he was not immune from persecution. If it is in the same manner he was sent that he too has sent us, then know that we are also not immune from persecution. The disciples must have received the shock of their lives at Jesus's answer when they asked what they stood to gain, having left all to follow him:

> Peter said to him, "We have left everything to follow you!"
>
> "I tell you the truth," Jesus replied, "no one who has left home or brothers or sisters or mother and father or children or fields for me and the gospel will fail to receive a hundred times as much in this present age (home, brothers, sisters, mothers, children and fields—and with them, *persecutions*) and in the age to come, eternal life." (Mark 10:26–30; emphasis added)

Jesus was blunt about it. He didn't mince words about the fact that the apostles would be persecuted. So friends, let no one hoodwink you with words tasting like fresh wine, full of sweetness but lacking in substance, that ministry is or will be a rosy ride.

Do you know that one of the earliest things God made Apostle Paul realize after his conversion was that he was going to be persecuted? "But the Lord said to Ananias, 'Go! This man is my chosen instrument to carry my name before the Gentiles and their kings and before the people of Israel. I will show him how much he must suffer for my name'" (Acts 9:15–16). Paul did not only come to accept it, he even longed for it! He wrote, "I want to know Christ and the power of his resurrection and the fellowship of sharing in his sufferings, becoming like him in his death" (Phil 3:10). And knowing that no sincere Christian can escape persecution, he told the church in Philippi, "For it has been granted to you on behalf of Christ not only to believe on him, but also to suffer for him" (Phil 1:29).

Still on persecution, let us go back and examine Matthew 10:17 more closely: "Be on your guard against men, they will hand you over to the local councils and flog you in their synagogues."

Be on Your Guard against Men

Here, Jesus warns us to be careful in our relationships with people. We must be on the alert. We must define our relationships and set appropriate boundaries. Any relationship (with males or females, believers or unbelievers) that you cannot define will defile you. I tell you, man is a potential devil. Paul's experience with Phygelus, Hermogenes, Demas, and Alexander the coppersmith, who greatly opposed the gospel, neatly underscores the importance of being on our guard against men. For more discussion on this topic, see the section on precaution, in chapter 2.

They Will Hand You over to the Local Councils

The reason why we are told to be on our guard against others is given—that people will betray us unless we are on our guard against them. Scripture warns that Satan may take advantage of us if we are not unaware of his devices. Man of God, I say to you today, beware of others taking advantage of you; beware that they can betray you. If Judas could betray Jesus, men will betray you.

The local council mentioned here symbolizes civil authority. It means that persecution will come from the government and her agencies through laws, policies, and statements. It is, therefore, not surprising that governments of nations and other forms of civil and political authority persecute Christians with relish and careless abandon.

And Flog You in Their Synagogues

Jesus was flogged, Paul was also flogged, many others have been, and many more will yet be flogged. But note that in this phrase, persecution will not come from civil authority but from religious institutions—the church in particular. Hence, Jesus said, "in their synagogues." By reference to synagogues, Jesus was telling the apostles to expect persecution from religious institutions, those claiming to have a better understanding of divine truths and to possess deeper insight and revelation.

Persecution from the church will come in form of "spiritual witchcraft"—strong manipulation. It will come from brethren, sincere Spirit-filled brethren. It will come from those who are strong adherents to the theory of "as it was in the beginning, so is now and ever shall be." They will suspend, excommunicate, or label you an agent of darkness. Jesus was persecuted in such a manner, and by the "church" in his day.

Now let's look at verse 18 wholly: "On my account you will be brought before governors and kings as witnesses to them and to the Gentiles." When Jesus said that on his account we will be brought before governors and kings as witnesses, I believe the Lord wants to drive it home that through persecutions he will bring us before the high and mighty in society for one purpose—as witnesses. Sadly, many ministers, instead of being witnesses to the crème de la crème of society go seeking financial and other forms of assistance from these men, or go wining and dining with them.

Our Attitude towards Persecution

Since persecution is inevitable for every minister, what should our attitude towards it be? Scripture, once again, has the answer:

> They called the apostles in and had them flogged. Then they ordered them not to speak in the name of Jesus, and let them go. The apostles left the Sanhedrin, rejoicing because they had been counted worthy of suffering disgrace for the Name. . . . They never stopped teaching and preaching the good news that Jesus is the Christ. (Acts 5:41–42)

The attitude of the apostles was one of joy. Persecution did not stop them; it should not stop you. They saw it as a privilege to be persecuted for the sake of Jesus's name. This was their attitude; it should be ours too.

The Benefits of Persecution

It looks absurd to be talking about benefits of persecution. But there are benefits attached to it. Of Jesus it was written, "Although he was a son, he learned obedience from what he suffered" (Heb 5:8). That means persecution helps one to become obedient. It is a practical way of learning obedience.

Secondly, persecution prepares you to share in his glory: "Now if we are children, then we are heirs—heirs of God and co-heirs with Christ, if indeed we share in his suffering in order that we may also share in his glory" (Rom 8:17). The effect of sharing in his suffering is that we may share in his glory. This means that we cannot share in his glory without sharing in his suffering. So persecution (suffering for the sake of Christ) gives us the privilege of being prepared to reign with Christ. First Peter 4:14–16, however, places a limitation on what we are to suffer for:

> If you are insulted because of the name of Christ, you are blessed, for the Spirit of glory and of God rests on you. If you suffer, it should not be as a murderer or thief or any other kind of criminal, or even as a meddler. However, if you suffer as a Christian, do not be ashamed, but praise God that you bear that name.

PROTECTION

The next storm-oriented P is *protection*. Verses 19 and 20 of our text tell us: "But when they arrest you, do not worry about what to say or how to say it. At that time you will be given what to say, for it will not be you speaking, but the Spirit of your Father speaking through you." This speaks of protection—divine protection. Though we shall be persecuted, God expects us to face it with the assurance that we shall be divinely protected. We shall not be overtaken or consumed by it. Jesus himself had experienced this, so he knew what he was talking about. Let's see what he said of himself: "For I did not speak of my own accord, but the Father who sent me commanded me what to say and how to say it. . . . So whatever I say is just what the Father has told me to say" (John 12:49, 51). Jesus also told us that he is with us every inch of the way (Matt 28:20). Whatever you are going through, just know that Jesus is there with you and his presence guarantees your protection.

Now, let's go a step further. A close look at verses 19 and 20 will show that the manifestation of protection is predicated upon two things: (a) the ability to hear the voice of the Spirit, and (b) the willingness to obey the Spirit.

With regard to the first, every believer ought to be able to hear the voice of the Spirit of God and be able to know the ways God speaks to him or her. The ministry greats have written so much on this; hence, I do not intend to dwell so much on it. (I think it is vital to suggest that you go through Kenneth E. Hagin's book, *How You Can Be Led by the Spirit of God*. That book in my opinion is the finest material on the subject.) But I do want to say that God will speak to you, not just to guide you but also to protect you. In fact, divine guidance is in itself protection, as it is shown in Isaiah, "Whether you turn to the right or to the left, your ears will hear a voice behind you, saying, 'This is the way, walk in it' " (Isa 30:21). The Psalmist says in Psalm 62:11, "God hath spoken once, twice have I heard this; that power belongeth unto God" (KJV). God spoke and the psalmist heard. Therefore, you should hear when he speaks.

As for the second, anytime you obey the things you hear from the Spirit, you are not only protected but you get unprecedented success. Friend, let this sink into you: persecution is an integral part of ministry because there is the guarantee of protection. Both are storm-oriented Ps. Psalm 121 is a classic example of a Scripture that mirrors divine protection.

PERSEVERANCE

Perseverance is the third storm-oriented P. Verses 21–31 expatiate on this, but let us begin by considering verse 21 and 22:

> "Brother will betray brother to death, a father his child, children will rebel against their parents and have them put to death. All men will hate you because of me, but he who stands firm to the end will be saved."

The effect of these verses, particularly verse 21, is that although we have the assurance of protection, there will yet be storms. In fact, protection will not eradicate the storms of persecution. Things will become tougher as families split and oppose each other. All—(the government represented by the local councils, the church represented by synagogues, and now families)—will hate you because of Jesus and his gospel.

Protection will not cause these challenges to disappear or fizzle out. Jesus had divine protection yet he suffered. Paul was divinely protected yet he was kept in chains, imprisoned, and flogged. Divine protection did not stop their persecution, and it will not stop yours. Persecution and protection are like Siamese twins. What therefore should we do? Jesus tells us, "But he who stands firm to the end will be saved" (Matt 10:22b). We are to endure, to persevere; otherwise, we will not be saved.

Jesus amplifies the need for perseverance in verses 23–31. He tells us in verse 23 to be ready to flee, that is, to make emergency exits. The reason for all these warnings is that he himself would go through the same things (see verses 24–25). Between verses 26 and 31, the Master charges us again to persevere as we go through trials and temptations, because our protection is guaranteed. We are told to go about our assignments boldly without fear of any power because our lives are in the hands of the Father and he alone determines what happens to us. He closes with these words, "So don't be afraid, you are worth more than many sparrows" (Matt 10:31).

Paul knew this and so admonished Timothy to "*endure hardness* as a good soldier of Jesus Christ" because "no man that warreth entangleth himself with the affairs of this life; that he may please God who called him to be a soldier" (2 Tim 2:3–4 KJV; emphasis added). Paul, in effect, was telling Timothy to persevere in the face of adversities.

Let's quickly bring this discourse on perseverance to a close by reminding ourselves again of some points. First, persecution is an integral part of ministry; therefore, it must come. However, the shape and shade in which it will come varies for each minister. Secondly, protection follows persecution. This is because God's divine plan is to ensure that we are not consumed by the persecutions that will confront us. Thirdly, divine protection does not eradicate persecution. Hence, we must persevere. Jesus was divinely protected while on earth, yet he did not escape persecution.

The life and experiences of Job, the servant of God, mirrors perfectly what we have been talking about here. Satan persecuted Job but could not take his life, as Job was divinely protected. This divine protection did not put an automatic stop to the persecution; Job had to go through it. As such, he had to persevere.

PROGRAM

The next P we shall discuss stands for *program*. When we say a thing is programmed, we mean it is designed to last for a specified time period. Its life span is predetermined. Verse 23 introduces us to this P:

> "When you are persecuted in one place, flee to another. I tell you the truth, you will not finish going through the cities of Israel before the Son of Man comes."

This verse makes it clear that persecution is not an endless affair. It will come to an end when the Son of Man comes. It is therefore programmed. This is because we already know its duration.

The issue of programming also extends beyond the storm-oriented Ps. It applies to the entire calling of ministers and their ministries. No ministry is designed to last forever. Jesus, the pattern Son, told us that ministry—the calling—is programmed to last for a time frame after which it becomes impossible to do it. Hear him, "As long as it is day, I must do the work of him who sent me. Night is coming, when no one can work" (John 9:4). In effect, the work is to be done in the day, not at night. Therefore, the time frame is already predetermined, already programmed.

Everything in life is programmed. Ecclesiastes 3:1–8 supports this view; however, a look at verse 1 will be sufficient for our purpose: "There is time for everything, and a season for every activity under heaven." Everything in life is programmed to occur at a particular time and to last for a certain duration.

Program as one of the Ps means that every assignment the minister is given has a set time for accomplishment. Else, he will be deemed a failure. Ministers should take great pains to seek out the timing of God for their lives and ministries, and they will not miss it. Of the children of Issachar, it was written that they were men with an understanding of the times and all their brethren were at their command, yet they were so few (1 Chr 12:32). It is not the size of the congregation, but your understanding of heaven's time frame for your ministry that matters. The Lord will help us. Amen.

4

The Reward-Linked Ps

GOD REWARDS the people he uses. He does not owe any person. The Scripture is clear on this:

> Therefore, my dear brothers, stand firm. Let nothing move you. Always give yourselves fully to the work of the Lord, because you know that your labor in the Lord is not in vain. (1 Cor 15:58)

> Behold, I am coming soon! My reward is with me, and I will give to everyone according to what he has done. (Rev 22:12)

The above passages show that God rewards his chosen people. He does not use people only to dump them later. But then, he has his standards, to reward everyone "according to what he has done." He tries the works of men by fire (1 Cor 3:12–15).

What we are about to discuss here are those things that qualify a minister to be rewarded and those things that can disqualify a minister from being rewarded. Apostle Paul told us that only those who run according to the rules would obtain the prize. Therefore, it is possible to finish the race and not obtain the prize because one did not run according to the rules.

Matthew 10 remains our text as we consider the last ten verses (32–42).

> "Whoever acknowledges me before men, I will also acknowledge him before my Father in heaven. But whoever disowns me before men, I will disown him before my Father in heaven.
>
> "Do not suppose that I have come to bring peace to the earth. I did not come to bring peace but a sword. For I have come to turn
>
> 'a man against his father,
>
> a daughter against her mother,
>
> a daughter-in-law against her mother-in-law—
>
> a man's enemies will be the members of his own household.'
>
> "Anyone who loves his father or mother more than me is not worthy of me; anyone who loves his son or daughter more than me is not worthy of me; and anyone who does not take his cross and follow me is not worthy of me. Whoever finds his life will lose it, and whoever loses his life for my sake will find it.
>
> "He who receives you receives me, and he who receives me receives the one who sent me. Anyone who receives a prophet because he is a prophet will receive a prophet's reward, and anyone who receives a righteous man because he is a righteous man will receive a righteous man's reward. And if anyone gives a cup of cold water to one of these little ones because he is my disciple, I tell you the truth, he will certainly not lose his reward.

PRIDELESSNESS

> Pride goes before destruction and a haughty spirit before a fall. (Prov 16:18)

> The Lord resists the proud but gives grace to the humble. (1 Pet 5:5)

God humiliated Nebuchadnezzar for seven years because of pride. Lucifer, son of the morning, lost his place in heaven as a result of pride. Pride is both a cankerworm and a cancer. It won't make you see your ignorance and folly until it destroys you.

Simply put, pride is the glorification of self. To declare it the opposite of humility is an aberration. Pride is the root cause of megalomania. It believes that humility is synonymous with humiliation. A humble person is not a humiliated person; rather, a proud person will certainly end up a humiliated person. Pride is self-glorification but to be prideless is to humble oneself in order to promote another. In verses 32 and 33, Jesus said, "Whoever acknowledges me before men, I will also acknowledge him before my Father in heaven. But whoever disowns me before men, I will disown him before my Father in heaven." Jesus's statements in the verses above are very instructive. According to our Lord, he will acknowledge (recognize and reward) people who, instead of promoting themselves, promoted him. Proud people cannot and will not do that for each other. They see themselves as the "be all and end all." The natural person wants to boost the ego, but Jesus expects his people to deny themselves and lift him up instead. This was what

John the Baptist meant when in John 3:30, he declared: "He must increase, but I must decrease."

Jesus, through these verses, gives us the basic criterion for recognition before the Father in Heaven: *acknowledging him before men on earth*. This I believe is the fire by which our works will be tried (1 Cor 3:11–15). Therefore, all who promote self and not Jesus will receive no reward or acknowledgement before the Father. The issue is not whether they labored in the Lord's vineyard, or had large followings, or healed the sick; the criterion for acknowledgement, for receiving heaven's reward, is acknowledging (glorifying) Jesus on earth.

Let this sink into you: the primary reason why many ministers will not receive any reward in heaven or would be mere spectators at the awards night in heaven will be because of pride. It would be because they became ambassadors of themselves instead of being Jesus's ambassadors on earth.

Ego is the reason why ministers do not acknowledge Jesus. Les Brown, motivational speaker and author of the bestseller, *Live Your Dreams*, speaking at one of the ManPower Conferences organized by the highly celebrated preacher, Thomas Dexter Jakes (better known as Bishop T. D. Jakes), said *ego* is an acronym, it means: edging God out! When people become proud, they feed their ego, that is, they edge God out of their lives and ministries. They become over-conceited, believing that success in life and ministry is a function of their abilities. But this, Jesus tells us, is at the risk of being a spectator at the awards ceremony in heaven.

A fundamental question that you need to provide an answer to, regardless of the scope of your ministries or the titles you go by, is whether you acknowledge Jesus before all others in everything you do. You need not think too far, the answer is right there in your heart. "How do I acknowledge or refuse to acknowledge Jesus?" If your ministry or work in the Lord's vineyard is not aimed at presenting Jesus to the people, you are not acknowledging Jesus. But if your ministry is aimed at presenting Jesus, then you are acknowledging him.

The issue of being prideless, as a prerequisite to being rewarded, means dying to self in order that Jesus may be seen and glorified. It is choosing to remain humble and hidden even though the flesh desires to be elevated and seen. Apostle Peter has this to say: "All of you clothe yourselves with humility toward one another, because, God opposes the proud but gives grace to the humble. Humble yourselves, therefore, under God's mighty hand, that he may lift you up in due time" (1 Pet 5:5–6).

PRICE

> "Do not suppose that I have come to bring peace on the earth. I did not come to bring peace, but a sword. For I have come to turn
>
>   'a man against his father,
>
>   a daughter against her mother,
>
>   a daughter-in-law against her mother-in-law—
>
>   a man's enemies will be the members of his own household.'

> "Anyone who loves his father or mother more than me is not worthy of me; anyone who loves his son or daughter more than me is not worthy of me; and anyone who does not take his cross and follow me is not worthy of me. Whoever finds his life will lose it, and whoever loses his life for my sake will find it." (Matt 10:34–39)

Every thing has a price! Freedom has a price, captivity has a price, sin has a price, and salvation has a price. The price may be tangible or intangible, consciously or unconsciously paid, but everything has a price attached to it.

In the six verses just quoted, Jesus explains the price of following him, of being his minister. A detailed perusal of these verses reveals that the price of following Jesus, of being his minister, of being a channel through which the anointing will flow, is a total (unconditional, unqualified) yielding to the cause of Jesus. This yielding, it must be noted, must be based on love; otherwise, it won't count.

In these six verses, we see that Jesus places a high level of importance on this standard. It is nonnegotiable. There is no alternative. This is so because Jesus declares that anyone who cannot jettison physical comforts, family relationships, or whatever he or she holds sacred is not worthy of him.

Many times we pray: "Lord take me higher, use me Lord." We scream, shout, and howl, banging the floor with our palms and feet in prayer. We take oaths and enter into covenants with God saying that we will not disappoint if and when he pours out the anointing on us. But the great explosion—the breakthroughs that we seek—never seem to come to pass. The reason is that we have yet to pay the price.

Without doubt, we've been engaged in long and protracted fasts; we've sown seeds upon seeds; given one "Isaac" after another; done all the things associated with price paying. Yet nothing happens.

Let me rock the foundation of your theology. All the above, and things associated with them, are not the price. They are the natural or physical manifestation of the price but not the price in itself. The Pharisees did these same things and still failed to meet God's standard. If these things were the price, then the Pharisees would have qualified. The gifts of the Spirit and the anointing are not a reward for spiritual or other pious activity. They are gifts of God's grace. You don't earn them, but you can attract them.

The price, as seen in the statements of Jesus in the verses under consideration, is a totally unconditional, self-sacrificing, comfort-denying, pleasure-jettisoning, death-embracing love for Jesus. The Master himself said:

> Anyone who loves his father or mother more than me is not worthy of me; anyone who loves his son or daughter more than me is not worthy of me; and anyone who does not take his cross and follow me is not worthy of me. Whoever finds his life will lose it, and whoever loses his life for my sake will find it.

Loving Jesus would necessitate placing him and the work of his kingdom above everything else. It is what will necessitate fasting, seed sowing, sacrifices, and prayers, not the other way around. It would also cause to die every dream and desire, aspiration and ambition that could mar your relationship with him.

Heaven has yet to release the great anointing, the great explosion, because we have yet to sincerely and unconditionally love the Lord Jesus first and above all things. Jesus's reply to the Pharisees (and Sadducees) on the question of what the greatest commandment in the law was speaks volumes of how seriously heaven takes this matter.

Hearing that Jesus had silenced the Sadducees, the Pharisees got together. One of them, an expert in the law, tested him with this question:

> "Teacher, which is the greatest commandment in the law?" Jesus replied, "Love the Lord your God with all your heart and with all your soul and with all your mind. This is the first and greatest commandment" (Matt 22:34–38).

The first and greatest command is to love God with the totality of our being. Jesus says, this is the first—*the foremost*—requirement God seeks from all people. It is also the greatest—that is, there is nothing above it or better than it.

The reason why there is so much talk but no power (in the body of Christ), so many principles, no anointing, is that, although we fast and pray, and we obey all the guidelines necessary to demonstrate the power of God, we do not really love the Lord. What many a minister loves is the glamour that goes with the anointing and the fame that comes with miracles and healings. We love to see the crowd flock to hear us talk about Jesus and his works. But we do not love the Lord. Remember, Peter followed Jesus for three and a half years, but at the end Jesus asked him, "Do you love me more than these?" Jesus wanted to know if Peter loved him more than the signs and wonders, more than the fame and glamour that Peter had gained by reason of his relationship with Jesus. The Master wanted to know what Peter's motivation was. It was so important to Jesus that he had to ask Peter this same question thrice.

If you are in a love relationship or caught in the web of emotions, or better still, married, think of the passion and excitement that engulfed the fabrics of your being when you first met and started going out with your loved one. Think of the many silly things you did just to demonstrate that love. Think of sacrifices made in order to be with your loved one. Friend, I urge you—think! Now I ask, is that the same kind of passion you have towards God, towards Jesus, towards kingdom matters, when you say and sing, "I love you Lord"?

Many of us are ready to shed blood (even our own blood), to keep our love relationship going but we are not ready to do the same for the love of Jesus. But Jesus in Matthew 22:38, tells us that loving God is the first (the numero uno) and the greatest. He rates every other love relationship as secondary, "And the *second* is like it; love your neighbor as yourself" (Matt 22:39; emphasis added). The love you have for your spouse, your children, your neighbors, your job, is secondary. That is how God rates it. Our love for Jesus is what should propel us to make sacrifices and adjustments. The price of following Jesus, of being his minister, and, finally, of being rewarded by him is to love him unconditionally. When there is an unconditional love for Jesus, going the extra mile for him and for his work won't be difficult. This is the price that qualifies you for a reward on earth and in heaven.

The price we need to pay is to love Jesus even at the risk of entropy in our relationships with our biological family members, at the risk of throwing to the dogs what this entire world holds sacred. When we are at this point, fasting, praying, making seed donations, and all that we do in the name of price paying become easy to carry out. It will be done, not as if we are attempting to bribe or pay for the anointing but to prepare ourselves for the Master's great use.

When the price is paid, heaven is opened to us, we do exploits in the name of Jesus, and we are assured of being there at the awards night in heaven.

PRIZE

After the price comes the prize (which is the last but by no means the least of the fifteen Ps for every minister). It is to this prize that we shall now direct our attention.

> "Whoever finds his life will lose it, and whoever loses his life for my sake will find it.
>
> "He who receives you receives me, and he who receives me receives the one who sent me. Anyone who receives a prophet because he is a prophet will receive a prophet's reward, and anyone who receives a righteous man because he is a righteous man will receive a righteous man's reward. And if anyone gives even a cup of cold water to one of these little ones because he is my disciple, I tell you the truth, he will certainly not lose his reward." (Matt 10:39–42)

A cursory look at the above passage shows that there are rewards (prizes) awaiting the prices paid for the Master's business. One also discovers that the prizes can be divided into two categories: those for ministers and those for the ministered-to.

The Minster's Reward

> Whoever loses his life for my sake will find it.
> (Matt 10:39b)

The price of following Jesus and of being his minister, we had earlier said, is to love him to the point of embracing death. Jesus, himself, confirmed it: "If anyone comes to me and does not hate his father and mother, his wife and children, his brothers and sisters—yes, even his own life—he cannot be my disciple" (Luke14:26). Did you see that? "Even his own life." The supreme price to be paid as ministers is our lives. No wonder the book of Hebrews tells us that we really have passed through nothing when we have shed no blood (Heb 4:4). But there is hope. The hope is that after every price is a prize. Verse 39b of our principal text tells us that we shall find the very life we gave up in the course of paying the price. This means that in place of the life lost, we get life in return.

It must nevertheless be emphasized that this is only possible if our lives were actually given up for the cause of the gospel of Jesus and not for any other thing. Hence, Jesus said, "for my sake."

The Reward of the Ministered-to

Between verses 40 and 42 is contained what I have called the reward for the ministered.

> He who receives you receives me, and he who receives me receives the one who sent me. Anyone who receives a prophet because he is a prophet will receive a prophet's reward, and anyone who receives a righteous man because he is a righteous man will receive a righteous man's reward. And if anyone gives even a cup of cold water to one of these little ones because he is my disciple, I tell you the truth, he will certainly not lose his reward. (Matt 10:40–42)

Here, the basis for being rewarded is for meeting the needs of ministers. Remember that earlier in our study, we said that God has made provisions to meet the needs of his ministers, but he has placed those provisions in the people. It is these people through whom God meets the needs of his ministers that he wants to reward. The basis for their reward is what is contained in the verses under consideration.

These persons will be rewarded because they assisted the ministers of God. The basis for which they so acted was because the apostles were ministers of God and nothing more. As such, Jesus says, they will certainly not lose their reward. The ministry of the those who ministered to the apostles (those with specific assignments) was so important that Jesus had to assure them of the reward for even giving a cup of water to the apostles. Therefore, even though these persons are not ministers in the sense in which we generally refer to ministers today, but may be referred to as the ministered, they will be rewarded for their labors in meeting the needs of ministers. You would better appreciate their importance if they were removed from the picture and the ministers had to, alongside their ministerial duties, engage in the search for food, clothing, and all other mundane things necessary for a comfortable life.

The combined effect of verses 39 through 42 is that every person will be rewarded, regardless of the cadre of ministry in which he or she functions—prophets (representing the five-fold) for being prophets, and the people (representing other members of the body of Christ) for assisting them. The cadre or placement is not the important factor. What is important is that individuals pay the necessary price, which is functioning in their place for the sake of the gospel of Jesus.

The certainty of the prize, which shall be given to us, is contained in Revelation 22:12: "And behold I come quickly and my reward is with me to give everyman according as his work shall be" (KJV). Jesus said he would come quickly to reward us. If he has not lied before and cannot lie—then, it means that our reward is sure. But then, note that he says: to reward everyman "according as his work shall be." This means the prize we will get is directly proportional to the quality of our work for him.

The quality of our work for him is not determined by our oratory prowess, stage and pulpit theatrics, organizational skills, the size of the crowd that listens to us each day, or any of those things that we, as humans, have contrived to assess and rate ourselves. It is, however, determined by the fulfillment of the purpose for which he pulled, prepared, pushed, powered, and provided for us.

All who do not take note of the caveat contained in Revelation 22:12 (as regards the basis for the kind of prize each man will receive) may end up in disappointment when they get the prize for their labor in heaven.

Conclusion

These then are the fifteen Ps for every minister:

   pull
   push
   place
   purpose
   power
   provision
   people
   precaution
   persecution
   protection
   perseverance
   program
   pridelessness
   price
   prize

I sincerely believe that you'll be blessed by the truths contained in this book and that your ministry will take a new turn for the better. As this book draws to a close, I leave you with this Scripture: 1 Timothy 4:15. If you follow the counsel of this Scripture, the sky becomes, not your limit, but your starting point.

Meditate upon these things; give thyself wholly to them; that thy profiting may appear to all. (KJV)

Practice and cultivate and meditate upon these duties; throw yourself wholly into them [your ministry], so that your progress may be evident to everybody. (AMP)

Suggested Reading

Abioye, David. *Stewardship: The Pathway to Honor*. Lagos, Nigeria: Dominion, 1993.

Agboga, Ehis. *A Future and a Hope*. Ibadan, Nigeria: Freedom Press, 2000.

Akanni, Gbile. *What God Looks for in His Vessels*. Gboko, Nigeria: Peace House, 1999.

Copeland, Kenneth. *Managing God's Mutual Funds—Yours and His*. Tulsa, OK: Harrison House, 1997.

Hagin, Kenneth. *How You Can Be Led by the Spirit of God*. Tulsa, OK: Kenneth Hagin Ministries, 1978.

Hagin, Oretha. *The Price Is Not Greater Than God's Grace*. Tulsa, OK: Faith Library, 1991.

Jacobs, Cindy. *The Voice of God*. Ventura, CA: Regal Books, 1995.

McGregor, Chip. "Mentoring." In *Stories for the Heart*, edited by Alice Gray, 105–106. Sisters, OR: Multnomah / Questar, 1996.

Oyedepo, David Olaniyi. *Towards Excellence in Life and Ministry*. Lagos, Nigeria: Dominion, 1992.

Ehis Agboga speaks to Christian ministers, leaders, and workers. He welcomes the privilege to speak in your church, fellowship, seminar, symposium, and conference.

E-mail: ehisagboga@yahoo.com
pastorehis@justice.com
Website: www.healingstreamsonline.org
Telephone: 234-805-645-5474

About the Author

Attorney-at-law, Bible teacher, evangelist, and pastor, Ehis Agboga is the founder and president of Healing Streams International Outreach, a ministry committed both to helping Christians enter into their God-promised destinies and Christian leaders pursue and maximize the call of God on their lives. Ehis also hosts the Ministers Advance Reformation Conference (MARC). A playwright, actor, and poet, the author is a firm believer in the practicability and relevance of God's word in today's world. Ehis and his wife, Pamela, make their home in Lagos, Nigeria's commercial capital.

For more information on the ministry and work of Ehis Agboga log on to www.healingstreamsonline.org

Other Books by Ehis Agboga

A Future and a Hope
Dare: Success within Your Reach

www.ingramcontent.com/pod-product-compliance
Lightning Source LLC
Chambersburg PA
CBHW070921160426
43193CB00011B/1547